AUTISM
UNDERSTANDING, SUPPORT & POSSIBILITIES

A Holistic Guide to Awareness, Inclusion, Independence and the Future of Autism Care

Devender Singh Sibbal, Govind Pathak

notionpress.com

INDIA · SINGAPORE · MALAYSIA

ISBN
Paperback 979-8-90479-524-5
Hardcase 979-8-90479-857-4

A Note Before You Begin

This book is written with deep respect for every individual on the autism spectrum, their families, caregivers, educators, and support communities worldwide. Its purpose is not to define anyone by a diagnosis but to foster understanding, inclusion, and empowered action.

Disclaimer

The information in this book is for educational and awareness purposes only. It does not replace professional medical, psychological, therapeutic, or clinical advice. Always consult qualified professionals for evaluation, diagnosis, and individualized support.

Author's Intent

Every effort has been made to present information responsibly, accurately, and compassionately. Autism research continues to evolve some frameworks or references may change over time as the field advances.

Therapies & Technologies

References to interventions, AI systems, or organizations are for general awareness only not endorsement or guaranteed outcomes.

AI & Future Perspectives

Sections on digital therapeutics and integrated platforms are exploratory and forward-looking not medical or regulatory recommendations.

Emotional Narratives

Stories and situations reflect common experiences to foster empathy and understanding across the autism ecosystem.

ⓘ The authors and publishers shall not be held liable for any direct or indirect consequences arising from the interpretation or application of the content in this book. Readers are advised to exercise informed judgment and seek professional guidance before making decisions related to healthcare, therapies, or education.

A Journey Through Understanding

This book was born from questions asked quietly by parents, educators, therapists, and caregivers searching for clarity. It explores autism not as an isolated diagnosis, but as a complete human journey: emotional, practical, educational, and societal. Written with deep respect for every family navigating this path.

DEVENDER SINGH SIBBAL & GOVIND PATHAK

What This Book Offers

More than an explanation of autism this is a framework for understanding, connection, and action. It bridges the gap between fragmented support systems and the integrated ecosystems that families truly need.

For Families & Caregivers

Early signs, diagnosis, parenting realities, and the emotional truth of raising a child on the spectrum.

For Educators & Therapists

Therapies, interventions, inclusive education strategies, and tools for supporting different learners.

For Innovators & Leaders

AI, technology, policy gaps, economics, and the future of connected autism support ecosystems.

> **"No individual should feel excluded because they experience the world differently. And no parent should feel they must walk this journey alone."**

Early Signs & Diagnosis

Therapies & Interventions

Education & Inclusion

Adolescence & Adulthood

Policy & Ecosystem

Technology & AI

ⓘ This book is not a replacement for professional guidance. It is a broader framework combining science, humanity, lived experience, and future thinking to move readers from awareness toward **understanding, acceptance, and action.**

About the Authors

The minds behind *Autism Understanding Support and Possibilities* are an industrialist with three decades of institution-building and a technologist at the frontier of AI and ethics, bringing together complementary visions united by a shared commitment to inclusive, human-centric progress.

Devendra Singh Sibbal

Industrialist, entrepreneur, and social advocate. Director of the Utsav Group with over three decades of leadership across Central India and beyond.

Govind Pathak

Technologist, author, and strategic thinker. Alumnus of BIT Mesra with over two decades in telecommunications, AI, and next-generation digital ecosystems.

Devendra Singh Sibbal

As Director of the **Utsav Group**, his strategic collaborations with Indian Hotels Company Limited (Ginger Hotels) and Hero MotoCorp reflect a vision focused on commercial growth and regional community infrastructure across Chhattisgarh and neighboring regions.

- Hospitality and real estate development
- Automotive and mobility ecosystems
- Agricultural logistics and cold-chain infrastructure
- Media, philanthropy, and social empowerment

Govind Pathak

A senior technology leader and frequent speaker at industry forums, his work spans **AI governance**, future telecom, cognitive infrastructure, and the convergence of science, philosophy, and intelligent technologies.

- *Entangled Realities* Amazon Global Bestseller in Metaphysics
- *Moral Code: Ethics at the Heart of AI*
- *6G Threshold* and *Crypto Blueprint*
- Analytical frameworks for neurodiversity and adaptive systems

The Collaboration: A Shared Mission

> Their partnership represents a unique convergence of industrial vision and technological insight united by a singular, pressing challenge.

The collaboration between **Devendra Singh Sibbal** and **Govind Pathak** for *Autism* was born out of a shared belief: the systems supporting the neurodivergent community require not incremental change, but a **complete reimagining**. Though their professional paths originated in different sectors, they found common ground in the need for a more structured, compassionate, and ethical framework for neurodiversity.

Industrial Vision

Devendra's expertise in building sustainable ecosystems across infrastructure, logistics, and community development grounds the work in practical, scalable impact.

Technological Insight

Govind's deep understanding of AI ethics and human-centric innovation ensures the framework is forward-looking, accountable, and structurally robust.

Shared Purpose

Together, they advocate for a world where inclusion is built into the very architecture of our social and professional lives beyond awareness, toward action.

ⓘ Their writing and research aim to bridge technological advancement with ethical responsibility, human meaning, and long-term societal impact making *Autism* both visionary and practical.

Table of Content

Understanding Autism A Complete Guide

A comprehensive, 40-chapter journey across ten parts from first realization to global frameworks exploring autism through the lenses of science, family, education, policy, technology, and human empowerment.

Awareness
Recognize needs and opportunities

Understanding
Comprehend concepts and context

Application
Practice skills across chapters

Empowerment
Integrate learning into action

Table of Contents At a Glance

This guide is organized into ten interconnected parts, each building on the last to form a holistic understanding of autism spectrum disorder.

Part I & II: Understanding Autism & Early Identification

Part I Seeing Differently

Chapter 1: The First Realization the moment a parent notices something unique about their child's development.

Chapter 2: What is Autism Spectrum Disorder (ASD)? definitions, spectrum breadth, and prevalence.

Chapter 3: The Neurodiversity Perspective reframing autism as a different, not lesser, way of experiencing the world.

Chapter 4: The Science Behind Autism genetics, neurology, and current research frontiers.

Part II Early Identification & Diagnosis

Chapter 5: Early Signs Every Parent Should Know behavioral markers from infancy through toddlerhood.

Chapter 6: The Diagnosis Journey navigating assessments, specialists, and timelines.

Chapter 7: Emotional Reality of Diagnosis grief, acceptance, hope, and the path forward for families.

> ⓘ Early identification before age 3 significantly improves long-term outcomes for children on the spectrum.

The earlier a family begins this journey with awareness and support, the more empowered they become to shape a positive trajectory for their child.

Part III & IV: Therapies, Interventions & Education

Chapters 8 through 17 form the practical core of this guide covering every major therapeutic approach and the full landscape of autism-inclusive education.

Behavioral Therapies

Ch. 8–9: Understanding intervention approaches and applied behavioral analysis (ABA), evidence-based strategies, and individualized behavior plans.

Speech & Communication

Ch. 10: Augmentative and alternative communication (AAC), language development milestones, and speech therapy frameworks.

Occupational & Sensory

Ch. 11: Sensory integration therapy, fine motor development, daily living skills, and creating sensory-safe environments.

Social & Emotional Skills

Ch. 12–13: Social skills training, emotional regulation, integrative therapies including music, art, and play-based approaches.

Ch. 14: Inclusive vs. Special Schools

Weighing the benefits of mainstream inclusion against specialized environments for different learner profiles.

Ch. 15: Autism-Friendly Classrooms

Designing physical spaces, routines, and sensory accommodations that help autistic students thrive.

Ch. 16: Role of Parents in Learning

Home-school collaboration, parent-as-therapist models, and advocacy within the education system.

Ch. 17: Technology in Education

Apps, assistive devices, AI tutors, and digital tools transforming how autistic children learn and communicate.

Part V & VI: Family, Society & the Path to Independence

Family & Social Life (Ch. 18–21)

→ **Parenting a Child with Autism**

Strategies for daily routines, emotional resilience, self-care for caregivers, and building a support network.

→ **Sibling & Family Dynamics**

Addressing the needs of neurotypical siblings, maintaining family balance, and fostering empathy at home.

→ **Social Inclusion & Public Awareness**

Community education, reducing stigma, and creating autism-friendly public spaces and social environments.

→ **Navigating Healthcare & Support Systems**

Finding the right specialists, managing insurance, coordinating multi-disciplinary care teams effectively.

Adolescence & Adulthood (Ch. 22–25)

Transition to Teenage Years

Puberty, identity, social complexity, and mental health support during adolescence.

Skills for Independence

Life skills training: cooking, budgeting, transportation, and self-advocacy.

Employment & Careers

Vocational training, supported employment, neurodiversity hiring programs, and workplace accommodations.

Supported Living Models

Group homes, independent living with support, and long-term care planning for adults on the spectrum.

Part VII & VIII: Policy, Economics & the Technology Frontier

Chapters 26 through 33 zoom out from the individual to the systemic examining how governments, economies, and emerging technologies shape the autism landscape.

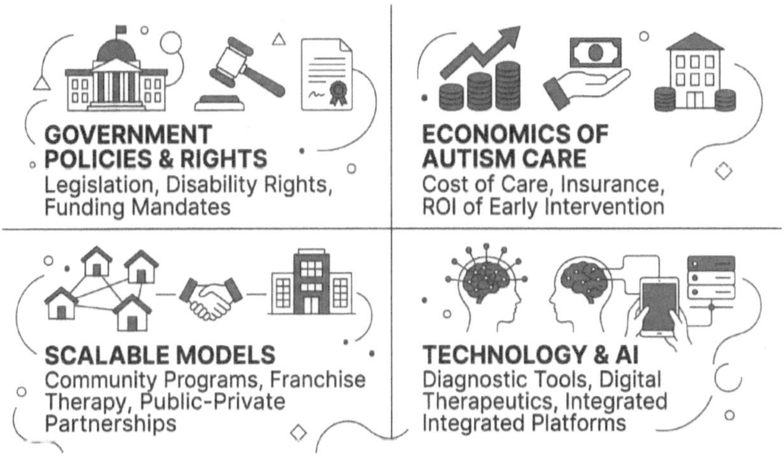

Policy & Economics (Ch. 26–29)

- **Ch. 26 Autism Ecosystem:** A systems-level view of how all stakeholders interconnect.
- **Ch. 27 Government Policies & Rights:** Disability legislation, IDEA, UN CRPD, and national frameworks.
- **Ch. 28 Economics of Autism Care:** Lifetime cost analysis, insurance gaps, and the economic case for early intervention.
- **Ch. 29 Building Scalable Models:** Replicable, affordable care delivery systems for diverse populations.

Technology & AI (Ch. 30–33)

- **Ch. 30 Role of AI in Autism Support:** Machine learning for early detection, personalized therapy, and progress tracking.
- **Ch. 31 Digital Therapeutics & Wearables:** Emotion-sensing devices, VR social skills training, and biofeedback tools.
- **Ch. 32 Building an Integrated Autism Platform:** Connecting diagnosis, therapy, education, and community in one ecosystem.
- **Ch. 33 Future of Autism Care:** Precision medicine, gene research, and the next decade of innovation.

Part IX: Action Handbook Who Does What

Chapters 34 through 37 translate everything in this guide into concrete, role-specific action plans. Whether you are a parent, educator, policymaker, or innovator, this section is your practical starting point.

Ch. 34 For Parents

A step-by-step guide from first concerns through diagnosis, therapy selection, school advocacy, and long-term planning. Includes checklists, resource directories, and self-care strategies.

Ch. 35 For Educators

Practical tools for creating inclusive classrooms, adapting curricula, collaborating with therapists, and supporting autistic students' social and academic growth.

Ch. 36 For Policymakers

Evidence-based recommendations for legislation, funding allocation, service delivery reform, and building national autism strategies that leave no one behind.

Ch. 37 For Startups & Innovators

Market opportunities, ethical design principles, partnership models with clinicians, and a roadmap for building technology that genuinely serves the autism community.

Each action handbook chapter includes ready-to-use frameworks, checklists, and real-world case studies to accelerate implementation.

Part X & Epilogue: A New Framework & The Road Ahead

From Fragmentation to Integration (Ch. 38–40)

Chapter 38 The Holistic Autism Framework proposes a unified model that integrates medical, educational, social, and technological dimensions of autism support into a single coherent system moving beyond siloed interventions toward whole-person care.

Chapter 39 India Blueprint: What Needs to Change examines the specific challenges and opportunities within the Indian context: workforce shortages, rural access gaps, cultural stigma, and the policy reforms needed to build a world-class autism ecosystem.

Chapter 40 Global Playbook synthesizes lessons from leading countries the US, UK, Israel, Singapore, and others — into a transferable framework that any nation can adapt to accelerate autism care at scale.

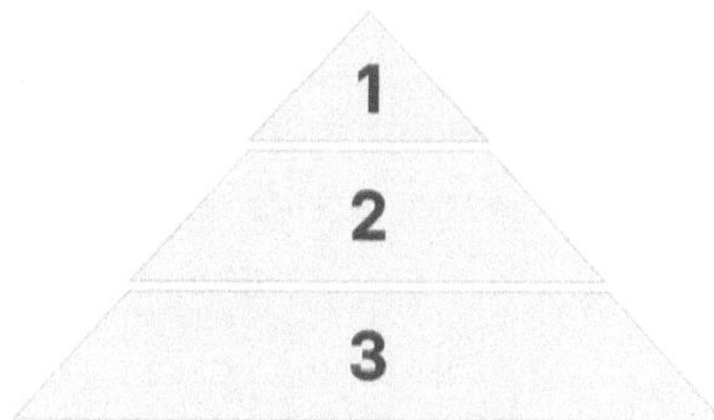

1 **Empowerment**

Agency, independence, full participation

2 **Acceptance**

Inclusion, belonging, neurodiversity

3 **Awareness**

Knowledge, early identification, understanding

> From awareness to acceptance to empowerment this is not just a progression of understanding, but a call to action for every stakeholder in the autism ecosystem.

Awareness

Understanding autism through science, stories, and lived experience

Early Action

Diagnosis, therapy, and education systems that respond quickly and effectively

Systemic Change

Policy reform, economic investment, and scalable models of care

Technology Integration

AI, digital therapeutics, and integrated platforms amplifying human support

Empowerment

Every autistic individual living a life of dignity, purpose, and full participation

This guide is an invitation to see differently, act boldly, and build a world where every mind belongs.

Chapter 1

The First Realization

It usually doesn't begin with a diagnosis. It begins with a feeling a pause that lingers a little longer than it should, a moment that doesn't quite fit the expected rhythm of childhood.

This is a space for that moment. For the uncertainty that quietly takes root before any words are found for it. And for the journey that follows.

The Moments That Collect

For many parents, the early days are filled with small, beautiful milestones first smiles, first sounds, first steps. These are the moments that build dreams. That create an invisible roadmap of what the future is supposed to look like.

But sometimes, the roadmap begins to blur. A child who doesn't respond to their name. Words that don't come or come and then disappear. A world that seems more comforting when experienced alone.

> These are not alarms. Not yet. They are just... moments. Moments that begin to collect.

The Reassurance That Doesn't Quite Settle

What Others Say

- "Boys speak late."
- "She's just shy."
- "He's very independent."
- "Every child is different."
- "He'll catch up."

What Stays With You

Advice comes easily from family, friends, even well-meaning strangers. And often, it comes with reassurance.

But reassurance has a strange way of coexisting with doubt. Because deep inside, something doesn't settle. It's not fear. Not immediately. It's something quieter. More persistent.

An instinct.

Learning to Notice

Parents begin to notice patterns that others don't. The way their child reacts or doesn't react to sound. The way routine becomes a necessity, not a preference. The intensity of certain behaviours that don't seem to follow typical boundaries.

Responses to Sound

An unusual sensitivity or an unexpected absence of reaction responses to sound can be one of the first patterns a parent notices.

Need for Routine

When routine shifts from preference to necessity, it can signal something worth paying closer attention to gently, without alarm.

Intensity of Behaviour

Certain behaviours that feel outside typical boundaries can be difficult to name but impossible to unsee once noticed.

The Quiet Comparison

And then comes comparison. Not out of judgement, but out of searching. At the park. At family gatherings. At school. Other children seem to move effortlessly through a world that your child is still trying to understand.

And somewhere in that quiet observation, a realization begins to form. Not fully. Not clearly. But enough to stay.

> Comparison is not a failure of acceptance. It is often how parents begin to find language for something they have sensed for a long time.

Living in the In-Between

This is often the most difficult phase. Not because of what is known but because of what is not. Uncertainty has a weight of its own.

Hope Holding on to the possibility that things will settle, that the questions will resolve themselves.	**Fear** The quiet dread that something significant is unfolding, even before there are words for it.
Resistance The deeply human impulse to protect a version of the future that once felt certain.	**Acceptance** A slow, non-linear shift not a single moment, but a gradual reorientation toward what is real.

In that space between these feelings, parents begin a journey they never planned for.

The Day of the Diagnosis

The day of the diagnosis, when it comes, is rarely dramatic. There are no cinematic pauses. No background music. No clear moment where everything suddenly makes sense.

Instead, it often unfolds in clinical language.

> **"Developmental delay."**

> **"On the spectrum."**

> **"Autism Spectrum Disorder."**

Words that are precise but not always understood. Words that carry weight but not always clarity.

And in that moment, parents are expected to process more than just information. They are processing identity.

Their child's. Their own. Their family's future.

> What does this mean? Will my child be able to speak? To go to school? To live independently? Did I do something wrong?

The mind searches for answers. The heart searches for stability.

Not the End A Different Beginning

Here is the truth that rarely gets said in that moment: **This is not the end of a journey. It is the beginning of a different one.**

Autism does not arrive as a single event. It unfolds. Through days that feel overwhelming. Through small victories that feel extraordinary. Through setbacks that test patience and strength.

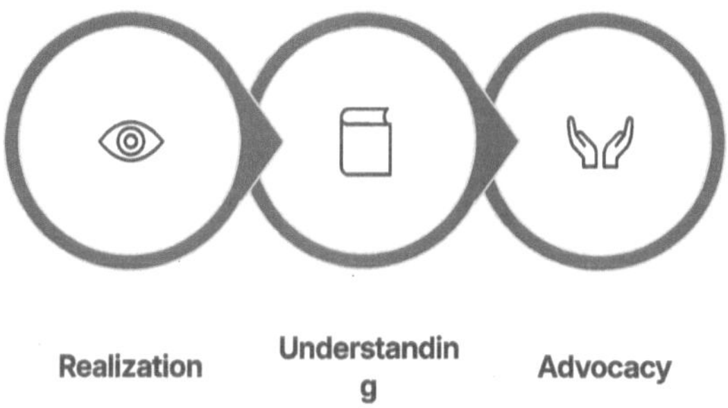

Each stage reshapes not just how parents care for their child — but how they see the world itself.

What Quietly Emerges

Within this journey, something else quietly takes shape. A deeper form of awareness one that cannot be taught in a classroom, but is lived day by day.

Celebrating Differently

Progress that others might overlook becomes the most meaningful kind a new sound, a moment of eye contact, a step into the unfamiliar.

Communication Beyond Words

Parents learn to read the language beneath language gestures, rhythms, silences and in doing so, draw closer to their child's inner world.

A Resilience That Is Lived

Strength is not declared it is built quietly, in ordinary moments that ask more than expected, and are met with more than imagined.

Where This Journey Truly Begins

This chapter does not offer solutions. It begins with understanding. Because before systems are designed, therapies are chosen, or interventions are applied there must be space to acknowledge what this moment truly is.

A Moment of Realization

The quiet understanding that something is different and that it matters.

A Moment of Uncertainty

The space between knowing and not knowing, where most parents quietly live for longer than anyone acknowledges.

A Moment of Possibility

Because difference is not something to be feared. It is something to be understood, supported, and deeply respected.

If you are reading this as a parent, you are not alone in this experience even if it often feels that way. The journey ahead will ask difficult questions. But it will also reveal unexpected strengths.

Chapter 2

What is autism spectrum disorder?

Once the word *autism* enters a parent's world, the instinct is to search for something precise a definition that explains everything. But autism resists neat boundaries. It challenges fixed categories. And yet, understanding it is essential, because **clarity is the first step toward meaningful support.** This chapter builds that foundation.

Beyond a Single Definition

Clinically, Autism Spectrum Disorder often referred to as **ASD is** defined as a neurodevelopmental condition that affects how a person communicates, interacts socially, and experiences the world around them.

This definition, guided by frameworks such as the **DSM-5**, provides a necessary medical lens. It helps professionals diagnose. It helps systems categorise. It helps policies define eligibility.

But for families, this definition often feels incomplete because it describes *what is observed*, not always *what is experienced.*

What the clinical lens offers:

- A shared language for professionals
- Access to diagnosis and support systems
- Eligibility for therapy and education resources
- A starting point not the whole story

Why It Is Called a "Spectrum"

One of the most important words in autism spectrum disorder is the word **spectrum** and it changes everything. Autism is not a single profile. It is a wide range of experiences, abilities, and challenges.

Fluent Speech, Social Nuance

Some individuals speak fluently but find social cues and implied meaning genuinely difficult to navigate.

Limited Verbal Communicatio n

Others may have limited or no verbal communication and rely on alternative ways of expressing themselves.

Exceptional Specific Abilities

Some display remarkable abilities in particular areas art, memory, mathematics, or music.

Lifelong Support Needs

Others require ongoing support in daily functioning and that support can make an extraordinary difference.

ⓘ There is no single "type" of autism. No uniform pathway. No standard trajectory. This is why comparisons between children and milestones often do more harm than good.

The Core Dimensions of Autism

While the expression of autism varies widely, differences are typically observed across two broad areas. Understanding these dimensions helps move us from confusion to compassion.

Social Communication & Interaction

- Difficulty understanding social cues
- Challenges maintaining conversations
- Differences in eye contact or facial expressions
- Limited use of gestures

This is not a lack of interest in connection it is a *difference* in how connection is expressed and understood.

Repetitive Patterns & Sensory Differences

- Repetitive movements such as hand-flapping or rocking
- Strong preference for routines
- Deep focus on specific interests
- Sensitivity to sound, light, texture, or touch

These are not "behaviours to eliminate" they are signals. Ways of coping, processing, and finding stability.

Prevalence: A Growing Reality

Across the world, autism is being identified more frequently than ever before. Understanding the scale and the gaps helps us recognise where support is most urgently needed.

1 in 36

Children Identified

Global estimates suggest approximately 1 in 36 children are identified on the autism spectrum.

↑

Rising Identification

Rates are increasing driven by broader awareness, improved screening tools, and more inclusive diagnostic criteria.

Late

Delayed Diagnosis

In many regions, children remain undiagnosed or are identified far later than ideal meaning early support is often missed.

In countries where awareness is still developing and access to specialists is uneven, the true prevalence is harder to measure not because autism is less common, but because the infrastructure for identifying it is still being built.

Myths That Continue to Persist

Despite growing awareness, autism remains surrounded by misconceptions. These myths do more than misinform they isolate families, delay support, and shape societal attitudes in ways that can be deeply harmful.

Myth: Autism is caused by poor parenting

Reality: There is no scientific evidence supporting this. Autism is a neurodevelopmental condition parenting style plays no role in its cause.

Myth: All autistic individuals have intellectual disability

Reality: Intelligence varies widely across the spectrum. Many individuals have average or above-average intellectual abilities.

Myth: Autism can be "cured"

Reality: Autism is not a disease. It is a neurodevelopmental difference. The goal is meaningful support not cure.

Myth: Autistic individuals lack emotions

Reality: Many experience emotions deeply sometimes more intensely than others. The challenge is often in expression, not feeling.

The Inner World of Autism

One of the most important shifts in understanding autism is moving from **external observation** to **internal experience**. What does the world actually feel like to someone on the spectrum?

- Hearing every sound at once, with equal intensity
- Struggling to filter background noise in a busy room
- Finding it difficult to interpret tone, sarcasm, or implied meaning
- Feeling overwhelmed by unpredictability

In such a world, behaviours begin to make sense. What may appear as withdrawal may actually be *self-protection*. What may appear as repetition may actually be *regulation*.

From correction

Reacting to the behaviour

To compassion

Understanding the experience

Understanding vs. Labelling and What Comes Next

A diagnosis can be genuinely helpful it can unlock access to therapy, education support, and vital resources. But it can also become limiting if it turns into a label that defines a child entirely.

> When we say *"a child with autism"*, we remind ourselves: **the child comes first.** The diagnosis is just one part of their story.

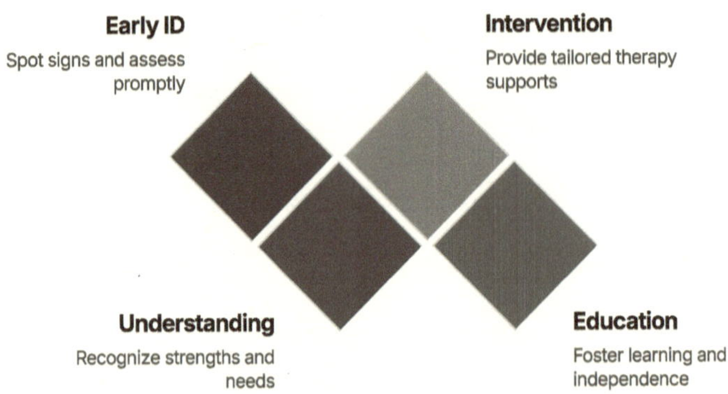

This chapter is not meant to provide all the answers it is meant to build a foundation. Because autism is complex, but it is not unknowable. The more clearly we understand it, the better we can support those who live it, every single day.

Clarity changes everything. With understanding, support becomes intentional, interventions become meaningful, and inclusion becomes possible.

Chapter 3

The Neurodiversity Perspective

There is a moment in this journey when something begins to change not outside, but within. It is not triggered by a report, a diagnosis, or a therapy plan. It begins with a single question: *What if we are looking at this the wrong way?*

From "Fixing" to"Understanding"

The Questions We Start With

How do we make the child speak? How do we reduce behaviours? How do we help them "fit in"?

These questions come from a place of care from love and a deep desire to help. But they share a common assumption: that something needs to be fixed.

A Quiet Realisation

Over time, many parents and increasingly, professionals begin to see something important.

> Not everything that is different needs to be fixed. Some things need to be understood.

A Different Lens

The concept of **neurodiversity** introduces a fundamentally different way of seeing. It suggests that variations in the human brain whether autism, ADHD, dyslexia, or others are not abnormalities, but natural variations. Just as biodiversity strengthens ecosystems, neurodiversity strengthens human society.

1. **Deficit**

   Something is wrong that must be corrected

2. **Difference**

   A natural variation to be understood

3. **Adaptation**

   Systems and people evolve together

This idea does not deny challenges. It does not romanticise difficulty. But it shifts the starting point profoundly and permanently.

The Power of Perspective

A Lesson from History

For decades, left-handedness was seen as a problem. Children were forced to switch hands. It was considered improper even wrong. Today, it is simply seen as a variation. Nothing to fix. Nothing to correct. Just different.

The neurodiversity perspective asks a similar question about autism: Are we trying to "correct" something that is fundamentally a different way of experiencing the world?

> ⓘ Perspective is not passive. The way we define something shapes how we respond to it in families, classrooms, clinics, and communities.

Voices That Were Not Heard

For a long time, conversations about autism were led almost entirely by clinicians, researchers, and caregivers important voices, but not a complete picture. What was missing were the voices of individuals on the spectrum themselves. And when those voices began to emerge, they brought something powerful:

> "We are not broken. We experience the world differently."

Thinking in Patterns

Many describe processing the world through patterns and systems rather than through language and narrative.

Feeling Deeply

Emotions are often experienced intensely but expressed in ways that others may not immediately recognise.

Needing Predictability

Structure and routine are not signs of rigidity they are genuine needs, not preferences.

These insights shifted autism from being *observed externally* to being *understood internally* a transformation that changed everything.

Strengths That Often Go Unseen

In a system that focuses heavily on challenges, strengths are easily overlooked. But many individuals on the autism spectrum demonstrate remarkable abilities that deserve recognition and cultivation.

Deep Focus

The ability to concentrate intensely on areas of interest, producing exceptional depth of knowledge and skill.

Pattern Recognition

Analytical thinking and the ability to detect complex patterns that others may miss entirely.

Direct Communication

Honesty and clarity in communication a strength in environments that value transparency.

Unique Problem-Solving

Unconventional approaches that generate innovative solutions in technology, research, and design.

The question is not whether these strengths exist. The question is whether our systems are designed to recognise and nurture them.

The Cost of a Narrow View

When Deficit Becomes Identity

When autism is seen only through a deficit-based lens, the consequences extend far beyond language. A child who is constantly told directly or indirectly that they need to be "fixed" may begin to internalise that belief. Over time, this can deeply impact confidence, self-worth, and mental well-being.

This shapes far more than how a child feels in a single moment. It influences:

- Educational approaches and expectations
- Employment opportunities in adulthood
- Social inclusion and belonging
- A person's sense of their own identity

> ⚠ Perspective is never neutral. How we define autism shapes how we respond to it and how individuals come to see themselves.

Acceptance vs. Support Not a Trade-Off

One common misunderstanding is that embracing neurodiversity means ignoring challenges. It does not. Acceptance does not mean absence of support.

Support Remains Essential

Speech therapy, behavioural support, and structured learning environments may all still be needed and are valuable.

But the Intent Changes

The goal is no longer to erase differences. The goal is to enable the individual to communicate, function, and thrive while respecting who they are.

> Neurodiversity does not say "do less." It says "do differently" with the whole person in mind.

Designing for Inclusion, Not Adjustment

Traditionally, the burden of adaptation has been placed on the individual: learn to behave this way, communicate this way, adjust to the system. The neurodiversity perspective asks a different question: **What if the system also adapts?**

Classrooms

Designed to accommodate different sensory needs lighting, noise levels, and flexible seating that allow every child to learn.

Workplaces

That recognise diverse cognitive styles and create environments where different thinkers can genuinely contribute.

Social Environments

That become more flexible, more patient, and more genuinely welcoming to people who experience the world differently.

> Inclusion is not about allowing someone to enter an existing system. It is about evolving the system itself.

A Bridge Between Two Worlds

Families often stand at the intersection of two perspectives that can feel in tension with one another.

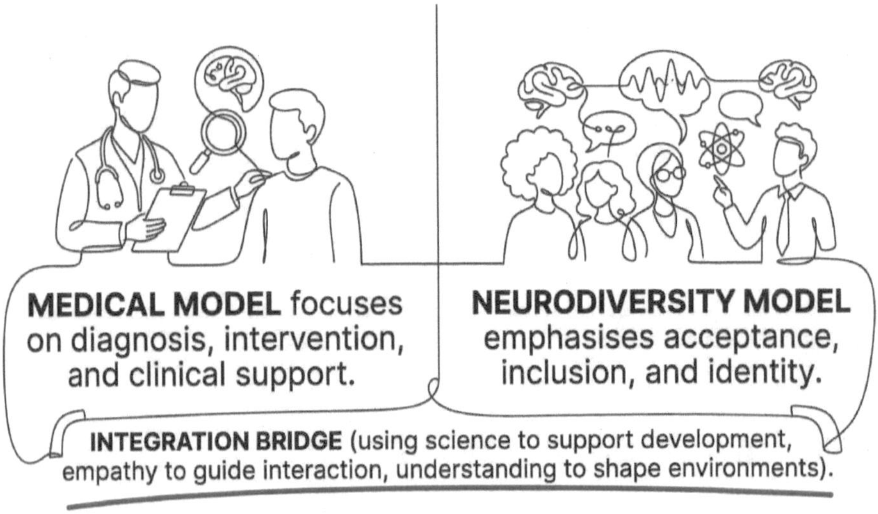

This can feel conflicting but it does not have to be. The most effective approach often lies in integration: using science to support development, empathy to guide interaction, and understanding to shape environments. These models are not enemies. They are complementary tools.

Why This Shift Matters

This is not just a philosophical debate. It has real-world implications for individuals, families, and society at large. When perspective shifts, everything it touches begins to change.

Therapy

Becomes more respectful of the individual's experience and identity

Education

Becomes more inclusive and designed for diverse ways of learning

Policy

Becomes more thoughtful and grounded in lived experience

Society

Becomes more humane and ultimately stronger for everyone

> Individuals on the spectrum are seen not as problems to solve but as people to understand.

Chapter 4

The Science Behind Autism

There comes a point in every parent's journey when emotion is no longer enough. Questions begin to demand deeper answers not just *what is happening*, but *why*. This chapter offers clarity rooted in science, so you can move from confusion and fear towards understanding and intention.

Let's Begin with What We Know

> Autism is **not caused by parenting**. Not by something you did. Not by something you didn't do.

For decades, families carried unnecessary guilt based on outdated theories that have since been firmly rejected by science. That weight was never yours to carry.

Today, research across the world points to a different understanding: autism is rooted in **how the brain develops and functions**. It is a neurological difference present from very early in life not a result of choices made, environments created, or love withheld.

Modern science has conclusively moved beyond blame. Understanding begins the moment we let go of it.

A Different Way the Brain Connects

The human brain is an extraordinary network billions of neurons forming trillions of connections. These connections shape how we process information, understand language, interpret social cues, and respond to our environment.

In individuals on the autism spectrum, these neural connections develop **differently** not incorrectly, not incompletely, but differently.

Over-Connected Pathways

May lead to intense focus, deep interests, or heightened sensitivity to the environment.

Under-Connected Pathways

Can make certain types of communication or sensory integration more challenging.

Unique Wiring

No two autistic brains are alike the spectrum reflects the extraordinary variety of human neurology.

Early Brain Development

Much of this wiring begins very early often before a child is even born. During pregnancy and the first years of life, the brain undergoes rapid, complex development. In autism, some of these processes follow a different trajectory.

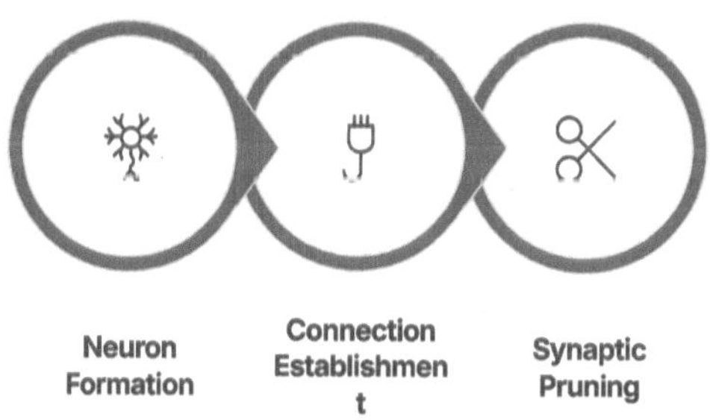

These developmental differences can influence how a child learns language, processes sensory input, and engages with the world around them. Crucially, these changes happen **long before any behaviour is visible** which is why autism is never something that appears suddenly.

Genetics: A Significant Piece of the Puzzle

One of the strongest areas of autism research points to genetics. Studies consistently show that autism tends to run in families, that **multiple genes** not a single one are involved, and that genetic variations can influence how brain development pathways unfold.

But genetics is not destiny. Not every child with a genetic predisposition develops autism. Instead, genetics provides a **probability framework** a set of possibilities, not certainties. It opens a door; it does not determine the outcome.

ⓘ Genetics explains *likelihood*, not inevitability. Many factors work together.

What Research Shows

- Autism runs in families at higher rates than chance
- Dozens of genes not one are linked to autism
- Genetic variations affect brain development pathways
- No single "autism gene" exists
- Twin studies show strong but not absolute heritability

The Role of Environment

Alongside genetics, researchers also study environmental influences. This does **not** refer to parenting or upbringing it refers to biological and developmental conditions such as prenatal health, maternal wellbeing, and early developmental environment.

Prenatal Conditions

Factors during pregnancy such as inflammation or hormonal changes may interact with genetic predispositions in complex ways.

Maternal Health

Research explores connections between maternal health conditions during pregnancy and developmental outcomes, though findings continue to evolve.

Multiple Interacting Factors

No single environmental cause has been identified. Autism results from a combination of genetic and environmental factors working together.

Science continues to evolve. Approach new claims with healthy curiosity and always consult trusted medical professionals.

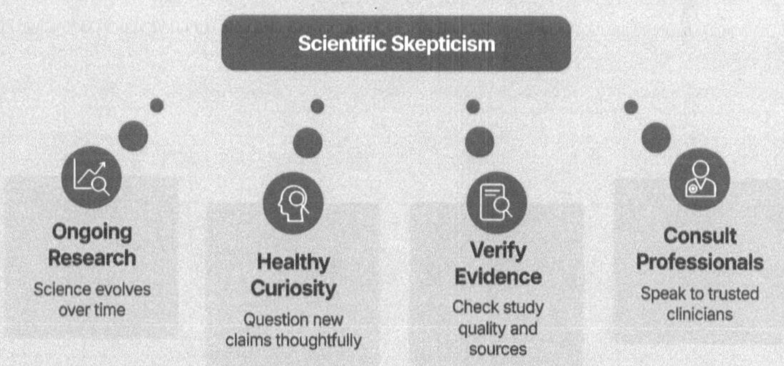

Understanding Sensory Processing

One of the most noticeable and most misunderstood aspects of autism is sensory experience. For many individuals on the spectrum, the world is simply not processed in a typical way. This is **not a behavioural issue**. It is a neurological one.

Sound

Sounds that others barely notice can feel overwhelmingly loud a busy classroom, a hand dryer, a crowded supermarket.

Light & Sight

Bright lighting or fluorescent bulbs can feel physically uncomfortable or even painful to some individuals.

Touch & Texture

Clothing labels, certain fabrics, or unexpected physical contact may cause real distress not fussiness.

Routine as Comfort

Predictable environments reduce sensory unpredictability which is why routines provide genuine neurological relief.

Why Behaviour Is Not the Whole Story

Autism is often recognised through behaviour. But behaviour is only the surface. Underneath every action is a neurological process and understanding that changes everything about how we respond.

Avoiding Eye Contact

May not mean disengagement it may mean the child is overwhelmed by the intensity of direct gaze.

Repeating Actions

May not mean rigidity repetitive movement is often a powerful self-regulation strategy.

Delayed Response

May not mean ignoring the child may be processing information at a different pace.

> When we understand the science, behaviour stops being confusing and starts becoming **meaningful**.

The Brain Is Not Fixed

Neuroplasticity

The brain's remarkable ability to change and develop over time especially in response to experience, learning, and support.

This is why early intervention is so powerful. Not because it changes *who* the child is, but because it supports *how* the brain learns and adapts.

What Becomes Possible

- Communication can improve and expand
- New skills can develop over time
- Greater independence can be built
- Confidence and connection can grow

Progress may look different for each child. But progress is **always possible**. The brain continues learning throughout life and so does every child.

Moving Beyond Fear

Understanding reduces fear.

Science can sometimes feel overwhelming complex terms, evolving studies, conflicting conclusions. But at its core, the science of autism offers something invaluable: a foundation for understanding.

1

We stop blaming

Science confirms that autism is not caused by parenting, vaccines, or life choices. Guilt loses its grip.

2

We stop guessing

Evidence replaces rumour. We begin to trust what research not fear tells us.

3

We respond with intention

Understanding the *why* behind a child's experience allows us to offer support that is thoughtful, targeted, and compassionate.

A Bridge to What Comes Next

This chapter was never meant to turn parents into neuroscientists. It was meant to offer just enough clarity to make sense of what might otherwise feel confusing or unpredictable.

1

Understanding the Brain

The science of *why* how neural wiring, genetics, and sensory processing shape your child's experience.

2

Recognising Early Signs

The knowledge of *when* what to notice, what to seek, and how early recognition opens doors.

3

Taking Timely Action

The confidence of *how* practical steps, trusted professionals, and the support that makes a difference.

> **Every behaviour has a reason. Every difference has a basis. And every child deserves to be understood not just observed**

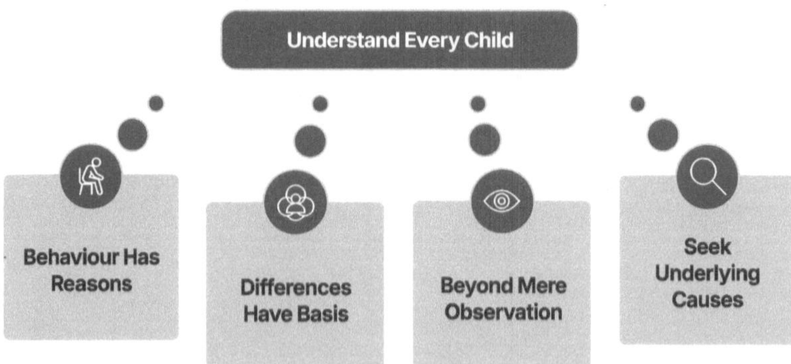

Chapter: 5

Early Signs Every Parent Should Know

There is a quiet power in noticing early. Long before a diagnosis is made, long before clinical terms are introduced, there are often small signals subtle, scattered, easy to miss. When seen together, they begin to tell a story. This chapter is about learning to read that story with clarity, compassion, and calm.

Why Early Signs Matter

Early childhood is a period of rapid brain development. Connections are forming. Skills are emerging. Foundations are being built. During this time, even small differences can become visible if we know what to look for.

Recognising these signs early does not mean rushing to conclusions. It means creating an opportunity to observe more closely, to seek guidance when needed, and to begin support at the right time. In autism, early awareness often leads to better outcomes not because we are trying to change the child, but because we are supporting their development when the brain is most adaptable.

Observe Closely

Pay attention to patterns across time and settings, not just isolated moments.

Seek Guidance

Reach out to professionals when questions arise early conversations are always worthwhile.

Begin Support

Start at the right time, when the brain is most adaptable and responsive to help.

Every Child Develops Differently And That's Okay

Before we go further, it is important to say this clearly: variation in development is entirely normal. Some children speak early. Some take more time. Some are naturally social. Some are more reserved. Not every delay is autism. Not every difference is a concern.

But **patterns matter**. **Consistency matters**. The **combination of signs matters**. And that is where awareness becomes truly valuable not as a tool for alarm, but as a guide towards understanding.

> ⓘ This chapter is not about finding something "wrong." It is about understanding something important so that support can begin at the right time.

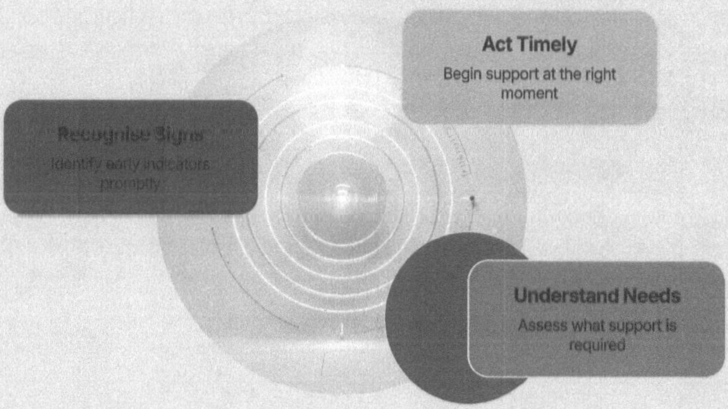

Early Signs in the First Two Years (0–2)

In the earliest years, signs can be subtle. They often appear not as clear problems, but as differences in response and interaction. Individually, any one of these may seem unremarkable. Together, they may begin to paint a picture worth exploring with a professional.

What Parents May Notice

- Limited or inconsistent eye contact
- Not responding to their name consistently
- Reduced social smiling
- Limited use of gestures such as pointing or waving
- Delayed babbling or vocalisation
- Less interest in interactive games like peek-a-boo

A Note on Playing Alone

Sometimes a child may seem content playing alone for long periods. At first, this can even feel like a strength a calm, independent child. But over time, the absence of shared attention the desire to engage with others can become more noticeable and worth exploring.

One sign alone is rarely enough. It is the pattern over time that matters most.

Signs in the Toddler Years (2–5)

As children grow, expectations around communication and social interaction increase. This is often when differences become clearer and more consistent. Signs tend to appear across four key areas.

Communication

- Delayed or absent speech
- Repeating words or phrases (echolalia)
- Difficulty starting or sustaining conversation
- Limited use of language for social purposes

Social Interaction

- Limited interest in playing with other children
- Difficulty understanding social cues
- Preference for solitary activities
- Reduced sharing of interests or experiences

Behavioural Patterns

- Strong attachment to routines
- Distress with small changes
- Repetitive movements such as hand-flapping or spinning
- Intense focus on specific objects or topics

Sensory Sensitivities

- Overreaction to sounds, lights, or textures
- Avoidance of certain environments
- Unusual responses to sensory input heightened or reduced

Regression: When Skills Seem to Fade

One of the more confusing and unsettling experiences for parents is regression. A child who was speaking a few words, making eye contact, and responding socially may suddenly seem to step back. Words disappear. Engagement reduces. Interactions that once felt natural become less frequent.

This can feel deeply worrying. But it is important to know: **regression is a recognised pattern observed in some children with autism.** You are not imagining it. And if this occurs, it is important not to wait. Seeking professional guidance early can make a meaningful difference.

⚠ If you notice a loss of previously acquired skills, do not delay. Speak to your child's paediatrician as soon as possible.

The Role of Parental Instinct

> Parents often sense something before they can explain it a feeling that something is not quite aligning. That instinct is valuable. Not because it is always correct, but because it is always worth exploring.

Too often, parental concerns are dismissed with well-meaning reassurances: *"Wait and watch." "He'll catch up." "She's just different."* Sometimes that is true. But sometimes, waiting delays support that could have helped much earlier.

Your concern is valid

A recurring worry is not anxiety it is attentiveness. It deserves to be heard.

Seeking help is strength

Consulting a professional is not overreacting. It is responsible, loving parenting.

Early action is kind

Even if concerns turn out to be nothing, exploring them early is always the right choice.

Cultural Realities: The Case of India

In many parts of India, recognising early signs comes with additional challenges that are important to acknowledge with empathy. Limited awareness among families, social stigma around developmental differences, delayed access to specialists, and a tendency to normalise or dismiss early concerns all play a role.

Extended families may offer reassurance with the best of intentions. Communities may discourage seeking professional help. As a result, diagnosis is often delayed. This delay is not due to a lack of care it is due to a lack of awareness and access. Which makes early education, exactly like this, so critically important.

Limited awareness

Many families are simply not yet informed about what early signs look like.

Social stigma

Fear of judgment can prevent families from seeking help they truly need.

Access to specialists

Development al specialists remain difficult to reach in many regions of India.

The power of education

Knowledge shared within communities can change outcomes for countless children.

What To Do If You Notice These Signs

Noticing signs is only the first step. The next step is action calm, informed, and timely. Here is a simple path forward that any parent can follow.

Remember: balance is key. Neither ignore what you are seeing, nor allow it to overwhelm you. You do not need all the answers right now you simply need to take the next step.

> Even if your child is later found not to be on the spectrum, early support never harms. Delay, however, can.

Early Support Is Not a Label It Is a Gift

One of the biggest fears parents carry

"What if I am labelling my child too early?"

This fear is understandable. And it is worth answering clearly and honestly.

Early support is about enabling, not labelling

If a child needs help with communication, providing that help early improves their outcomes. If a child needs support with sensory regulation, introducing strategies early reduces their distress. The goal is never to define who a child is it is to give them what they need to flourish.

We respond earlier

When the brain is most open to learning and growth.

We support better

With strategies tailored to the child's actual needs.

We reduce future challenges

By addressing difficulties before they compound over time.

Looking Ahead: From Signs to Clarity

In the next chapter, we move from recognition to clarity. From signs to diagnosis. Because while early signs raise questions, diagnosis begins to provide answers and with answers comes the ability to act with intention and confidence.

> Awareness is not about fear. It is about readiness. And readiness is the first step towards meaningful support.
>
> 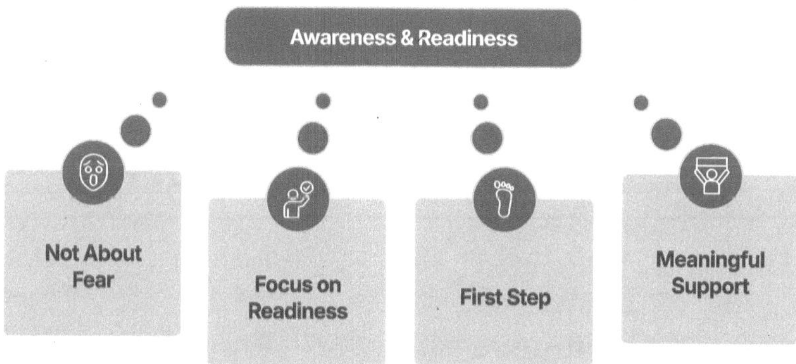
>

Chapter: 6

The Diagnosis Journey

There is a moment when observation turns into action. The signs have been noticed. The questions have been asked. The uncertainty has lingered long enough. This chapter walks families through the path toward diagnosis what it looks like, what to expect, and how to hold steady through each stage.

Taking the First Step

It starts with a decision

For many families, this moment arrives after hesitation. After reassurances from others. After second-guessing your own instincts. After hoping things might simply resolve on their own.

But eventually, the need to understand outweighs the fear of knowing. And the journey begins.

> The need to understand outweighs the fear of knowing. That is the moment the journey truly begins.

There is no perfect time to seek clarity. But seeking it even when it feels daunting is one of the most courageous things a parent can do. You are not alone in this step, and you do not have to take it alone.

Where Does One Start?

The path is not always linear, but it typically begins with one of these professionals. Each brings a different lens some focus on physical development, others on behaviour and cognition, others on neurological patterns.

Paediatrician

Often the first port of call. They monitor developmental milestones and can make referrals for specialist assessment.

Developmental Paediatrician

Specialises in child development and is trained to identify developmental differences, including autism.

Child Psychologist or Psychiatrist

Assesses behaviour, cognition, and emotional patterns. Plays a key role in formal diagnostic evaluation.

Neurologist

Consulted in some cases to rule out or identify co-occurring neurological conditions alongside the assessment.

Ideally, diagnosis is not the opinion of a single professional but the outcome of a multi-disciplinary assessment. Multiple perspectives lead to a more complete picture.

Screening vs. Comprehensive Diagnosis

It is important to distinguish between two stages in the diagnostic process. Screening and formal diagnosis serve different purposes and understanding the difference helps set realistic expectations.

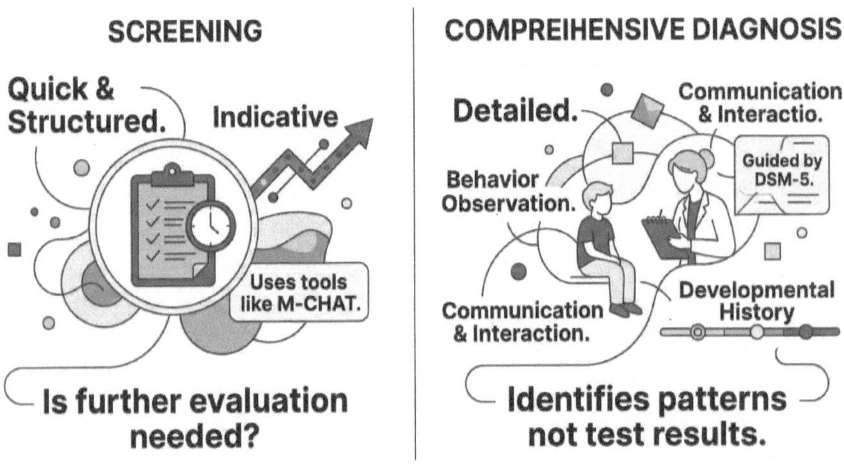

Autism is not identified through a blood test or scan. It is identified through patterns of behaviour and development which is why the comprehensive assessment process requires time, expertise, and careful observation.

What the Assessment Looks Like

For parents, the assessment process can feel unfamiliar even unsettling. It is helpful to know what to expect before you arrive. Professionals are not looking for right or wrong answers. They are looking for patterns.

Structured Play Sessions

The child engages in guided play while professionals observe social interaction, communication, and imaginative behaviour in a natural-feeling setting.

Developmental History

Parents and caregivers are asked detailed questions about milestones, early behaviours, and family context. Your observations matter deeply here.

Standardised Tools

Tools such as the ADOS (Autism Diagnostic Observation Schedule) provide a consistent framework to identify patterns across different assessors and settings.

The Waiting Period and the Moment of Diagnosis

The Wait

Between assessment and diagnosis, there is often a waiting period and it can be one of the most difficult phases. Uncertainty remains, but now it feels more immediate. Questions intensify: *What will they say? What if it is autism? What if it is not?*

This is where emotional support becomes critical. Many parents find themselves revisiting memories, reinterpreting behaviours, and quietly preparing for possibilities. That is a completely natural response.

> You do not have to process this alone. Connecting with other families or a counsellor during this time can make a meaningful difference.

The Moment

When the diagnosis is finally shared, it rarely feels routine even if expected, even if prepared for. The words carry weight.

> "Your child is on the autism spectrum."

For some, it brings clarity finally, an explanation. For others, it brings a wave of emotion. There is no single correct reaction. Some parents feel relief. Others feel grief. Most feel a combination of both. All of these responses are valid.

What Diagnosis Is and What It Is Not

A diagnosis is a starting point, not a conclusion. Understanding what it does and does not mean helps families move forward with clarity and confidence.

What a Diagnosis *Is*	What a Diagnosis Is *Not*
• A framework for understanding your child's needs • Access to therapies, resources, and support services • A shared language with educators and professionals • A starting point for intentional, informed action	• A prediction of your child's future • A limitation on their potential or possibilities • A complete definition of who they are • A reason to stop believing in what they can achieve

Autism is a spectrum, and trajectories vary widely. The risk lies in overinterpreting the diagnosis in assuming it determines everything that follows. It does not. It is a guide, not a ceiling.

From Diagnosis to What Comes Next

Once the diagnosis is given, one question becomes central: **What do we do now?** This is where many families feel unprepared because while a diagnosis provides a label, it does not always provide a roadmap.

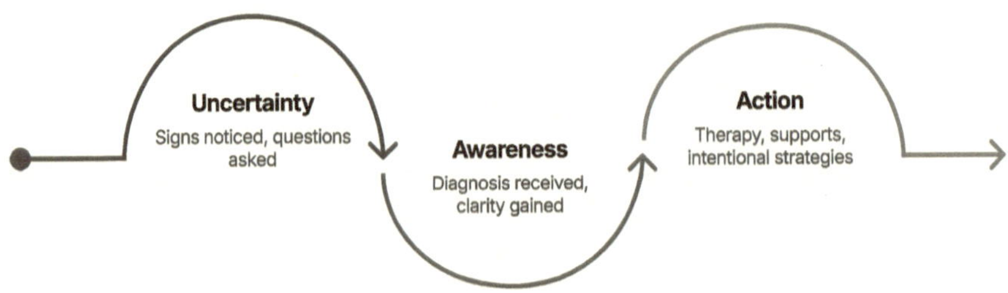

In the chapters ahead, we will move into the next phase exploring interventions, therapy options, and structured support systems. Because diagnosis answers *what.* But what matters next is: **How do we support? What truly works? What makes a meaningful difference?**

> A diagnosis does not define a child. But it can help define the support they receive. When used wisely, it becomes not a label but a guide.

Chapter: 7

The Emotional Reality of Diagnosis

A diagnosis does not arrive alone. It brings with it a wave of emotions, questions, and quiet realisations that are often difficult to put into words. For many families, this chapter is not about science or systems. It is about something far more personal. It is about **how it feels**.

When the Words Settle In

The moment of diagnosis may last only a few minutes. But its impact unfolds over days, weeks, sometimes years.

At first, there is often stillness. A pause as if the mind needs time to catch up with what has just been said. Then slowly, emotions begin to surface.

Not in a straight line. Not in a predictable order. But in waves.

> The diagnosis is a doorway. What lies beyond it takes time to see.

The Many Faces of Response

Every parent's journey is different. But there are emotional patterns that many experience sometimes all at once, sometimes in succession.

Shock

Even when suspected, hearing it confirmed can feel overwhelming. *This is real now.* The mind takes time to absorb what the ears have heard.

Denial

A natural protective response *Maybe this is a mistake. Maybe they will outgrow it.* Denial is not weakness. It is the mind's way of processing change.

Grief

Not for the child, but for expectations. The imagined future. The milestones that may look different now. This grief is often silent and often misunderstood.

Relief

Now we understand. Now we can act. For some, diagnosis brings clarity. Relief does not cancel out other emotions it coexists with them.

Fear

Perhaps the most persistent emotion. Will my child be independent? Will they find acceptance? These questions are real and they deserve space.

The Invisible Weight Parents Carry

Beyond emotions, there is a deeper layer one that is rarely visible from the outside. Parents often find themselves taking on multiple demanding roles simultaneously, even as their own feelings are still settling.

Advocate

Speaking up for a child's needs in schools, clinics, and communities often without a roadmap.

Researcher

Sifting through therapies, studies, and advice to find what truly helps.

Daily Therapist

Embedding therapy into every meal, routine, and moment of play at home.

Coordinator

Managing appointments, therapists, schools, and care decisions all at once.

ⓘ All of this happens while emotions are still settling. That is not a sign of failure it is a sign of extraordinary love.

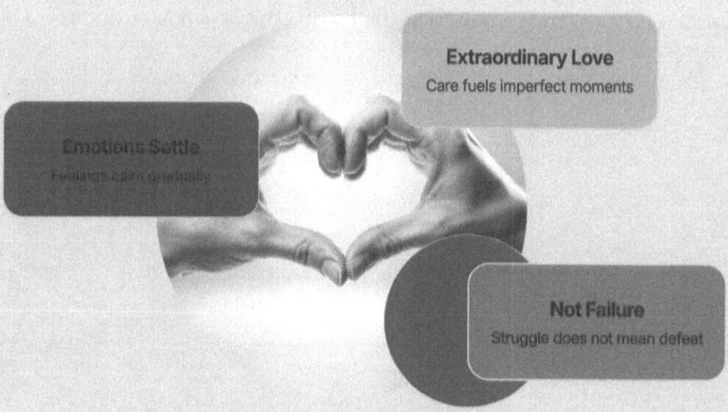

The Impact on Family Dynamics

Autism does not affect only the child. It touches the entire family system parents, siblings, and extended family each experience their own version of the journey.

Between Parents

- Differences in coping styles may emerge
- One may accept faster, another may take more time
- Open communication becomes critical

Siblings

- May feel confusion, curiosity, or neglect at times
- May take on responsibility early
- Often develop deep empathy and maturity

Extended Family

- Reactions can vary widely
- From warm support to misunderstanding
- Families must manage others' perceptions too

Social Realities: Navigating Stigma

In many communities, the emotional journey is layered with additional challenges. Social stigma, fear of judgment, and pressure to appear "normal" can make an already difficult time even harder.

Parents may hear well-intentioned but isolating words:

> "Don't label the child."

> "He will be fine."

> "Why tell others?"

While often well-meaning, these responses can deepen isolation. What families need most in this moment is **understanding, not dismissal**.

The Turning Point: From Reaction to Acceptance

Acceptance is not a single moment. It is a process a gradual, sometimes non-linear shift from *Why is this happening?* to *How do we move forward?*

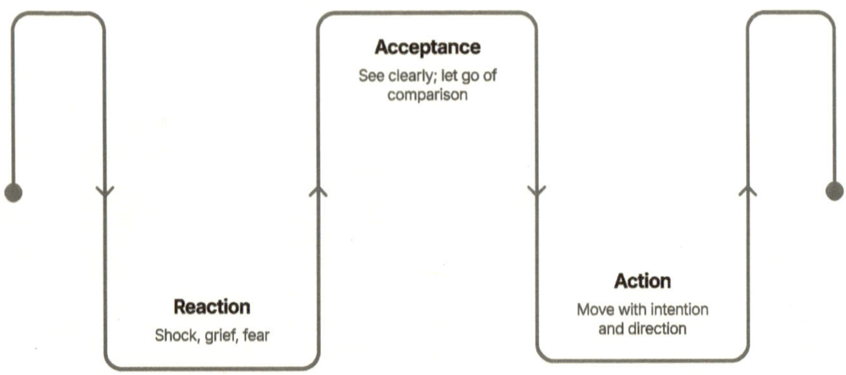

Acceptance does not mean giving up. It means seeing clearly, letting go of comparison, and beginning to act with intention. It is the turning point where energy moves from emotion towards direction.

Acceptance is not the end of feeling it is the beginning of moving forward with both heart and purpose.

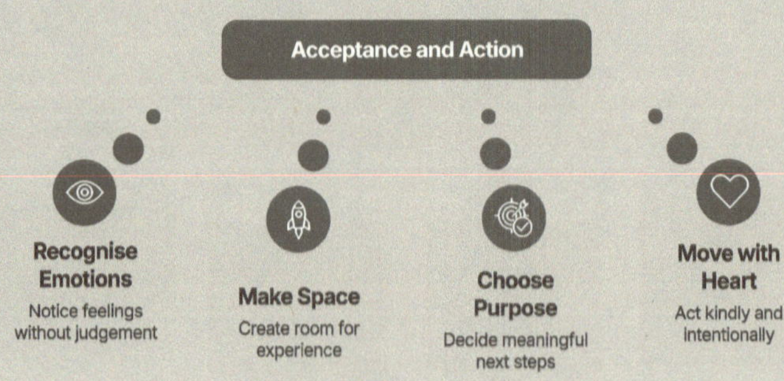

Building Support and Looking Ahead

No family should navigate this journey alone. Support takes many forms, and even one understanding voice can make a profound difference. Equally important is remembering to care for the caregiver.

Finding Your Support

- Other parents on similar journeys
- Therapists and trained professionals
- Online or local support groups
- Friends who listen without judgement

Caring for Yourself

- Take breaks when possible
- Seek your own emotional support
- Acknowledge your feelings without guilt

> Understanding led to diagnosis. Diagnosis led to emotion. **Now, emotion must lead to action.** That is where the next phase begins.

Chapter: 8

Understanding Intervention Approaches

After a diagnosis, one question begins to dominate everything else: **What should we do now?** It feels simple. But in the world of autism, it rarely has a simple answer. This chapter is here to help you move from overwhelm to understanding and from confusion to direction.

The Overwhelm of Options

The moment families begin exploring interventions, they encounter a flood of information therapies, programmes, methods, and claims. Some promise rapid improvement. Some suggest complete transformation. Some contradict each other entirely.

Suddenly, instead of clarity, there is confusion. Parents find themselves asking which therapy is best, how many hours are needed, and what happens if they choose the wrong one. This is not just a medical decision it feels like a defining choice. You are not alone in feeling this way, and there *is* a way through.

> ⓘ It is completely normal to feel overwhelmed at this stage. Most families do. The goal of this chapter is to give you a clear, calm framework not more noise.

There Is No One-Size-Fits-All

One of the most important truths to understand early is this: **no single therapy works for every child.** Because no two children are the same.

Different Needs

Every child has a unique profile of challenges that require tailored support.

Different Strengths

What one child excels at may be a significant challenge for another.

Different Responses

What works well for one child may have little effect on another.

This is why intervention must be **personalised, not standardised.** The best plan is one that is built around your child their specific needs, their strengths, and your family's circumstances.

The Goal of Intervention

A CRITICAL MINDSET SHIFT

Not the Goal

To make the child "normal." To correct who they are. To meet an external standard of development.

The Real Goal

To support the child in living a fuller, more confident, more connected life on their own terms.

Intervention is about enabling not correcting.

Before choosing *how* to intervene, it is important to understand *why.* When the purpose is clear, decisions become less overwhelming and more intentional.

- Communicating effectively
- Managing daily life with confidence
- Engaging meaningfully with others
- Navigating their environment safely

Two Broad Categories of Intervention

In the vast landscape of autism therapies, approaches broadly fall into two categories. Understanding the difference helps you ask better questions and make more informed decisions.

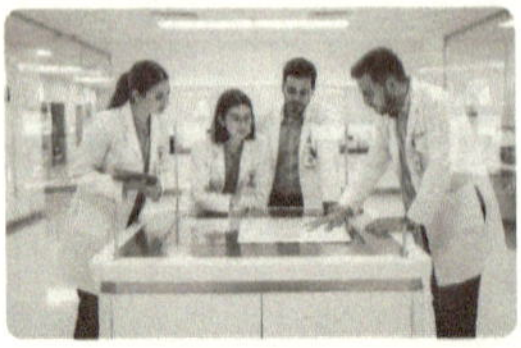

Evidence-Based Interventions

These therapies are supported by research and clinical studies. They have defined methodologies, measurable outcomes, and professional training standards. Examples include behavioural therapy, speech therapy, and occupational therapy. These form the foundation of most structured intervention plans.

Alternative or Emerging Approaches

These include diet-based interventions, supplements, experimental therapies, and non-clinical programmes. Some families report benefits; others see little change. Scientific evidence may be limited or inconsistent which means they should be approached with caution and informed judgement, not dismissed outright.

The Risk of False Promises

In a space filled with urgency and hope, there is also vulnerability. Families often encounter claims such as "guaranteed improvement," "quick results," or "complete recovery." These can be deeply tempting because they speak directly to a parent's deepest desire: to help their child as quickly and effectively as possible.

⚠ Autism is complex. Development takes time. If a claim sounds too good to be true, it is worth pausing and seeking a second opinion from a qualified professional before investing time, money, or hope.

This is not about being cynical. It is about protecting your family from approaches that may waste precious time and resources or worse, cause harm. Thoughtful scepticism is a form of advocacy for your child.

Intensity, Balance, and the Role of Play

How Much Therapy Is Enough?

Some programmes recommend intensive schedules many hours per week. Structured intervention is important. But balance is equally critical. Children are not only shaped by therapy sessions; they are shaped by *life itself.*

- Time to play freely
- Time to rest and recover
- Time to simply be themselves

Progress Beyond the Session

Progress is not measured only by structured sessions. It is also shaped by everyday experiences a shared laugh, a quiet routine, a moment of connection at the dinner table.

More hours does not always mean more progress. Quality, consistency, and joy all matter enormously.

You Are Not Just a Bystander

THE ROLE OF THE PARENT

Intervention does not happen only in therapy centres. It happens at home in daily routines, in small interactions, in the moments between formal sessions. Parents become active participants in the process. Not as professionals, but as consistent, emotionally connected guides.

Encourage Communication

Respond to every attempt to communicate words, gestures, sounds. Consistent responses build confidence.

Create Predictability

Predictable routines reduce anxiety and help children feel safe enough to learn and grow.

Respond with Patience

Emotional safety matters. A calm, patient presence at home reinforces everything formal therapy introduces.

The Missing Link: Coordination

One of the biggest challenges families face is fragmentation. A child may be attending speech therapy, occupational therapy, and behavioural sessions each with different professionals, different approaches, and different goals. Without coordination, efforts can become disconnected and even contradictory.

Intervention works best when it functions as a **system** not isolated parts. Ask your child's team how they communicate with one another, and advocate for regular joint reviews of your child's progress plan.

Access and Reality: The Indian Context

In India, intervention is often shaped by practical constraints that are rarely acknowledged in international guides. Families face a unique set of realities that require honest recognition not judgement.

Limited Professional Availability

Trained specialists are concentrated in urban centres, leaving many families with few local options.

High Cost of Therapy

Consistent therapy can be financially prohibitive for many families without insurance coverage or subsidy.

Geographic Disparities

Rural families may travel long distances for sessions, adding stress and limiting consistency.

This makes it even more important to focus on **high-impact interventions, parent-led reinforcement at home, and the most efficient use of available resources.** Doing what you can, with what you have, is always enough to start.

Redefining Progress

One of the most important shifts for parents is learning to redefine what progress looks like. It may not always be dramatic. It may not look like what you imagined before the diagnosis.

> Progress may look like a new word spoken, a longer moment of eye contact, reduced distress in a familiar situation, or a small but confident step toward independence. These changes may seem small but they are deeply meaningful.

1

New Word

Even one new word is a breakthrough worth celebrating.

1

Moment of Calm

One fewer meltdown in a stressful situation is real, measurable growth.

∞

Small Steps

Over time, small consistent steps add up to profound change.

From Confusion to Direction

The purpose of this chapter has not been to prescribe a specific therapy plan. It has been to create clarity and to help you move from overwhelm to understanding.

1. **Overwhelm**
   Too many options, too little guidance
2. **Understanding**
   A clear framework for evaluating choices
3. **Direction**
   Thoughtful, consistent, informed action

The next chapters go deeper into specific interventions, including behavioural approaches, communication therapies, and sensory and developmental support. Intervention is not about choosing perfectly. It is about **choosing thoughtfully** and then staying consistent, patient, and informed.

> You do not need all the answers today. You only need to take the next right step and you are already doing that by being here.

Chapter: 9

Behavioural Therapies: Understanding, Not Controlling

This Chapter explore autism support journey explores one of the most visible and most misunderstood aspects of raising a child on the spectrum: behaviour. This chapter reframes how we see, interpret, and respond to behaviour, offering a compassionate foundation for the approaches ahead.

What We See and What We Don't

Behaviour is often the most visible part of autism. It is what others notice first what teachers point out, what strangers sometimes misunderstand. But behaviour is not the full story. It is the surface.

A Need

The child may be seeking something essential comfort, clarity, or connection and behaviour is the clearest path available to them.

A Difficulty

Sensory overload, unclear instructions, or sudden change can create genuine distress that surfaces as visible behaviour.

A Way of Coping

Repetition, withdrawal, or intense reactions are often self-regulatory the child's way of managing what feels unmanageable.

A Form of Communication

When words are not available, the body speaks instead. Behaviour carries meaning that deserves to be heard, not simply silenced.

ⓘ A child may not always be able to say, *"This is too loud"* or *"I am overwhelmed."* So the body speaks instead through repetition, withdrawal, or intensity.

From "Fixing Behaviour" to Understanding It

Traditional approaches often focused on a single goal: reduce unwanted behaviour. But over time, a more meaningful understanding has emerged. Behaviour is not something to eliminate it is something to **interpret**.

> When we only try to stop behaviour, we may silence the signal without ever addressing the reason behind it.

The Old Question

"How do we stop this?"

Focused on eliminating the visible behaviour as quickly as possible, often without exploring the underlying cause.

The Better Question

"What is this behaviour trying to tell us?"

Shifts the focus toward understanding creating a foundation for lasting, meaningful change that respects the whole child.

Applied Behaviour Analysis (ABA): What Parents Should Know

ABA is one of the most widely used approaches in autism support. It is structured, systematic, and goal-oriented built on the principle that behaviour is shaped by environment and experience.

Break Skills Into Steps

Complex skills are divided into small, manageable parts so the child can build confidence at each stage without becoming overwhelmed.

Reinforce Positive Behaviours

When a child uses a word to request something, that behaviour is encouraged and celebrated building communication over time.

Reduce Interfering Behaviours

Behaviours that make learning difficult are gently addressed not by suppression, but by building alternative skills and strategies.

ABA can be a powerful tool when applied thoughtfully. **How it is delivered matters as much as the method itself.** Always look for approaches that respect your child's individuality and emotional experience.

The Ongoing Conversation Around ABA

While ABA has helped many children develop important skills, it is also an area of thoughtful, ongoing discussion. Autistic individuals, advocates, and researchers have raised concerns worth understanding not to discourage you, but to help you ask the right questions.

Concern: Rigidity

Overly structured approaches may feel restrictive to some children, particularly when flexibility and creativity are not built in.

Concern: Compliance vs. Understanding

A focus on "correct" behaviour without exploring emotional experience may prioritise surface outcomes over genuine wellbeing.

Concern: Individuality

Every child is different. A method that works well for one child may not suit another and good practitioners recognise this.

Modern ABA is evolving. Many practitioners now integrate autonomy, emotional attunement, and meaningful skill-building into their work. When evaluating any programme, ask: **Is this designed around my child or around a generic outcome?**

Meltdowns Are Not Tantrums

> One of the most important distinctions you will ever learn as a parent.

Tantrum

- Often goal-driven the child wants something specific
- The child typically retains some awareness of their surroundings
- May stop when the goal is achieved or attention is withdrawn
- The child often has control over starting and stopping

Meltdown

- Overwhelm-driven the child is unable to cope
- The child is not trying to control the situation they are losing the ability to process it
- Cannot be "negotiated" out of in the moment
- Requires safety, calm, and reduced stimulation

During a meltdown, what is needed is not correction it is **support**. Calm presence, reduced stimulation, and a safe space are the most powerful responses available to you.

The Power of Routine and Environment

Many children on the autism spectrum find deep comfort in predictability. Routine is not rigidity it is **stability**. Knowing what comes next reduces anxiety and creates a sense of control in a world that can often feel unpredictable and overwhelming.

Routine Reduces Uncertainty

Consistent daily rhythms mealtimes, bedtime, transitions help children anticipate what is coming and feel safe within their day.

Environment Shapes Behaviour

A supportive environment reduces triggers, encourages positive behaviour, and creates natural opportunities for learning and connection.

Smoother Transitions

Behavioural strategies use visual cues, warnings, and preparation to help children move between activities without distress.

Importantly, behavioural therapy is not confined to a clinic. It extends into home, school, and everyday interactions. **Consistency across these moments matters more than intensity in isolated sessions.**

The Heart of Behavioural Therapy

At its best, behavioural therapy is not about control. It is about **connection**. The goal is never to create "perfect behaviour" it is to support functional, meaningful interaction with the world.

For the Child

Communicate needs, navigate challenges, and build independence one meaningful step at a time.

For the Parent

Understand behaviour more deeply, respond with intention, and create environments where your child can truly thrive.

Looking Ahead

Chapter 10 turns to communication giving behaviour a voice, and exploring how children connect and express themselves beyond words.

> When we understand behaviour, we stop reacting and start responding. And in that shift, real progress begins.

You are not alone in this journey. Every insight you gain, every moment you choose understanding over reaction, is a gift to your child.

Chapter 10

Speech and Communication

There is a moment every parent waits for imagined long before it arrives. The first word. For many families, it comes naturally. For others, it takes time. And for some, it does not come in the way they expected. This chapter explores what communication truly means for children on the autism spectrum, and how families can support their child's unique voice whatever form it takes.

When Words Do Not Come

At first, the absence is subtle. A delay. A pause. A quiet waiting. Reassurance comes easily from others, from within. "Maybe a little more time." "Some children speak late."

But as months pass, the silence begins to feel different. Not empty but uncertain. And slowly, a deeper realisation emerges: **communication is happening, but not always in the ways we expect.**

> ⓘ A child who pulls your hand toward something they want, or cries when something feels wrong, is communicating. The message is there even when the words are not.

Pulling a hand

Guiding a parent toward a desired object or place

Crying or withdrawing

Signalling distress when something feels wrong

Looking, not pointing

Showing interest without yet sharing it verbally

Feeling deeply

Experiencing emotion without the words to express it

Communication Is More Than Speech

One of the most important shifts in understanding autism is this: **communication is not limited to spoken language.** A child who does not speak is not necessarily non-communicative. They may simply be communicating differently. The challenge is not always that communication is absent it is that it is not yet shared or understood.

Gestures

Pointing, reaching, waving intentional movements that carry real meaning

Facial Expressions

Smiles, frowns, and looks of surprise communicate feelings vividly

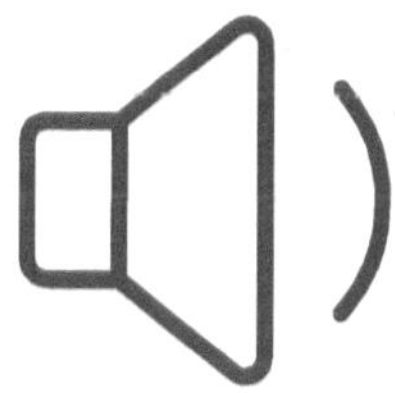

Sounds

Vocalisations, humming, or tones that signal a child's inner state

Body Movement

Posture, proximity, and physical actions that convey needs and reactions

Behaviour

Actions that serve as messages when other channels are not yet available

The Gap Between Understanding and Expression

In many children on the autism spectrum, there is often a gap between what they understand and what they can express. Some children may understand far more than they can say. Others may struggle with both.

What They May Understand

- Complex instructions given at home
- Emotional shifts in those around them
- Routines, patterns, and expectations
- Words and phrases heard regularly

What May Be Harder to Express

- Needs and wants in the moment
- Feelings of discomfort or confusion
- Responses to questions or prompts
- Social exchanges and conversation

> Imagine knowing exactly what you want to say but not having the words to express it. This is not silence. It is effort without output

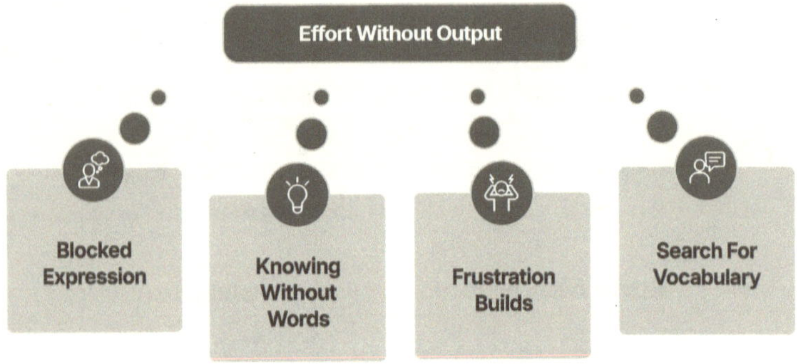

t.

Why Speech Develops Differently

Speech is not a single skill. It is a complex integration of multiple abilities working together. In autism, any one of these components may develop on a different timeline or in a different way. This is why speech development is not simply about "teaching words." It is about supporting an entire system.

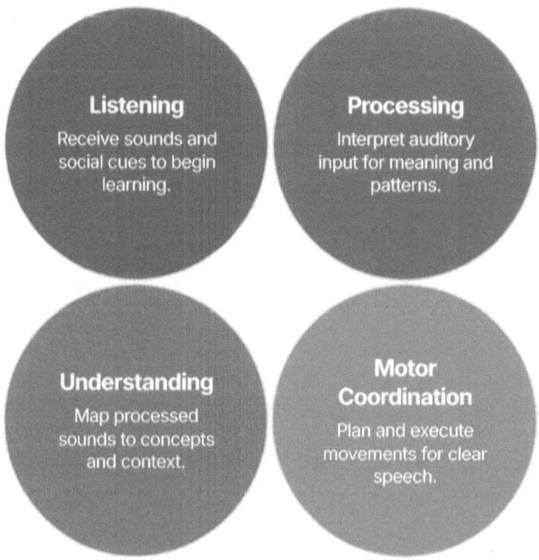

A child may hear sounds clearly but struggle to interpret meaning. They may understand words but find it difficult to produce them physically. Or they may speak fluently but not yet use language in social ways. Each profile is unique and each requires a tailored approach rather than a one-size-fits-all solution.

Echolalia: Repetition With Meaning

One of the most misunderstood aspects of speech in autism is **echolalia** when a child repeats words, phrases, or entire sentences, often from things they have heard before. At first, this may seem like imitation without understanding. But in many cases, echolalia is a meaningful step toward communication.

Language Processing

Repetition can be how a child works through and internalises heard language

A Way to Respond

When original language is difficult, echoed phrases fill the gap

A Bridge

Echolalia can serve as a stepping stone between listening and speaking spontaneously

What sounds repetitive may actually be meaningful just not in a typical form. Echolalia is often a sign that language is being absorbed, not ignored.

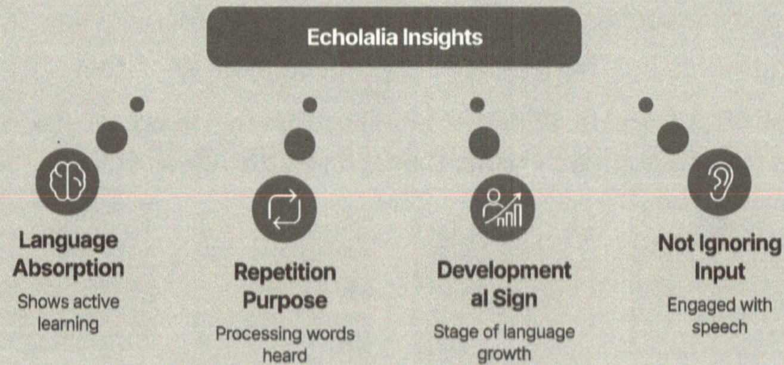

When Communication Breaks Down

When a child cannot express their needs clearly, something else often takes over: **behaviour**. Not because the child wants to act out but because communication has broken down and behaviour becomes the only available voice.

> *"I need help but I don't know how to say it."*

Understanding this reframes everything. A child who is crying, withdrawing, or becoming aggressive is not being difficult. They are communicating the only way they currently can. The message is there. Our task is to hear it.

Crying

An expression of overwhelm, discomfort, or unmet need

Withdrawal

A retreat from a situation that feels too demanding or confusing

Aggression

Frustration that has built beyond the child's ability to contain it

Repetitive actions

Self-regulation in the absence of another outlet

The Role of Speech Therapy

Speech therapy is one of the most important supports available in autism but its purpose is often misunderstood. It is not only about teaching a child to speak. It is about helping the child **communicate effectively**, in whatever way works best for them.

Building Language Understanding

Helping children make sense of words, instructions, and context around them

Encouraging Expressive Communication

Supporting the child in sharing needs, feelings, and ideas in any form

Developing Social Communication

Practising the back-and-forth of interaction, turn-taking, and shared attention

Supporting Alternative Communication

Exploring tools and strategies when spoken language needs extra support

Progress may be slow. But it is foundational. Because communication changes everything relationships, learning, independence, and wellbeing

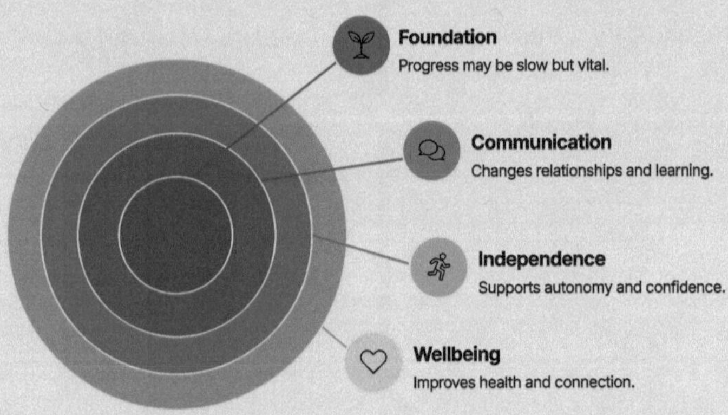

When Words Are Not the Only Path

Not all children will develop spoken language in the same way and for some, **Augmentative and Alternative Communication (AAC)** becomes essential. This is not a lesser path. It is simply a different one.

What AAC Can Include

Picture Systems

Visual symbols representing words, needs, and actions

Sign Language

Manual signs that bridge expression and understanding

Communication Devices

Digital tools that generate speech or text on the child's behalf

Will AAC stop my child from speaking?

This is one of the most common concerns parents express. Research and lived experience suggest otherwise. In many cases, AAC **supports** speech development by reducing frustration and building a child's confidence and intent to communicate. The goal is not speech alone. The goal is expression.

The Power of Being Understood

One of the most transformative moments in this journey is not always the first word. It is the **first time a child feels understood**. When a gesture is recognised, a sound is interpreted, a need is met without struggle something changes. Frustration reduces. Connection increases. Communication begins to flow — not perfectly, but meaningfully.

1

Gesture recognised

A point, a reach, a look met with understanding

1

Sound interpreted

A vocalisation heard and responded to with care

1

Moment of connection

Child and parent sharing the same understanding at last

> The first word matters. But the first moment of true connection that is where the journey truly begins.

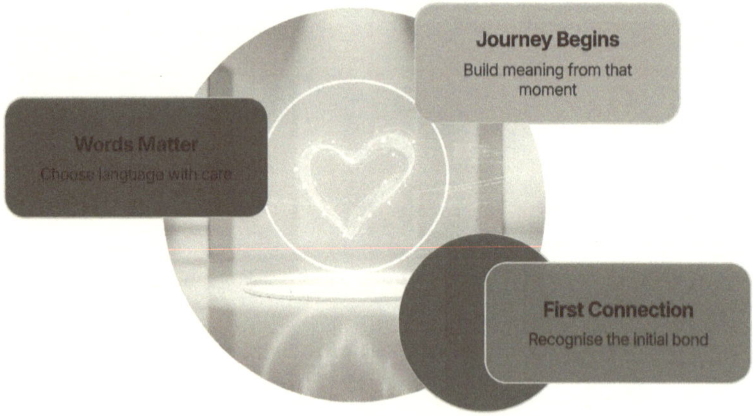

The Role of the Parent

Speech therapy may happen in sessions — but communication happens everywhere. At home. At mealtimes. During play. In the quiet moments between. **Parents are the most consistent and powerful communication partners a child has.**

You do not need to be a therapist to make a difference. Small, everyday interactions build something enormous over time.

Respond to attempts

When your child reaches, vocalises, or gestures — respond warmly and consistently. Every response teaches them that communication works.

Encourage interaction

Follow your child's lead during play. Comment on what they are doing. Pause and wait. Create space for them to contribute.

Create opportunities

Offer choices. Pause before helping. Let needs arise naturally so your child has a reason to communicate.

Small interactions build confidence. And confidence builds communication. You are already doing more than you realise.

Cultural Context: The Reality in India

In many parts of India, speech delays are often normalised. "He will speak later." "Boys speak late." While sometimes true, this mindset can quietly delay intervention — and early support significantly influences outcomes.

Access to trained speech therapists may also be limited, particularly outside of major cities. Rural families may face additional barriers of distance, cost, and awareness.

⚠ Normalising delay is not the same as understanding it. If a concern persists, seeking an assessment is always the right step — not the worried one.

Raise Awareness

Share what you learn with family members who may hold outdated beliefs about speech development

Seek Government Resources

NIMH, NIEPMD, and district early intervention centres offer assessments and therapy support

Use Teletherapy

Online speech therapy has expanded access significantly for families in smaller cities and towns

Redefining the Milestone

Perhaps the most important shift is this: **communication is not defined by words alone. It is defined by connection.**

Every one of these moments is a milestone. Every one of these moments deserves to be celebrated — as fully and as joyfully as a first spoken word. Communication is not a single destination. It is a thousand small arrivals, each one meaningful.

Every Child Has Something to Say

The journey is not about forcing words but about finding the voice that works for them.

Communication opens the door to interaction. But interaction requires more than language. It requires understanding social cues, emotions, and relationships.

In the next chapter, we move into that space — the world of **social connection and emotional development.** Because once a child has a voice, the next question becomes: how do they use it to connect with the world around them?

This Chapter	Next Chapter
Speech, communication, and finding a voice in any form	Social connection and emotional development building bridges to the world

Chapter 11

Occupational Therapy & Sensory Integration

Making sense of the world for children on the autism spectrum, everyday sensory experiences can feel vastly different. This chapter explores how sensory processing works, why certain behaviours arise, and how Occupational Therapy can help children find balance, comfort, and confidence in daily life.

When the World Feels Too Much or Too Little

We often assume that everyone experiences the world in similar ways. That sound is sound. Light is light. Touch is touch. But for many children on the autism spectrum, this simply isn't the case.

Over-stimulated

- Too loud
- Too bright
- Too fast
- Too unpredictable

Under-stimulated

- Not stimulating enough
- Not noticeable enough
- Not engaging enough

This is not behaviour. It is **sensory processing** and understanding it changes everything.

Understanding Sensory Processing

Every moment, our brain receives a constant stream of information from the senses sight, sound, touch, smell, taste, and movement. For most people, the brain filters and organises this input automatically and effortlessly.

In autism, this filtering process may work differently. Some inputs are amplified. Some are reduced. Some are difficult to organise. The child's response may appear unusual but it is, in fact, a natural and honest reaction to how they are experiencing the world around them.

Sight

Flickering lights or visual clutter may feel overwhelming.

Sound

Background noise may feel as loud as a direct conversation.

Touch

A clothing tag or light brush may register as intense discomfort.

Movement

The body may crave or resist physical input and motion.

Why Small Things Can Feel Very Big

> Imagine trying to focus on a conversation whilst every background sound feels equally loud or trying to sit still when your body constantly needs to move.

A buzzing fan. A flickering light. A crowded room. Things that go unnoticed by others can feel genuinely overwhelming. What we observe as "difficult behaviour" is very often a response to sensory overload the child's nervous system doing its best to cope.

The Body Seeks Balance

When sensory input becomes too much or too little the body instinctively seeks regulation. Spinning, jumping, rocking, and pressing against surfaces are not random. They are attempts to **self-regulate** and create stability in a world that feels unpredictable.

Behaviour Is Communication

Before reacting to a behaviour, pause and ask: *What might this child be feeling right now?* Understanding the sensory experience behind the behaviour transforms how we respond with empathy rather than correction.

What Is Occupational Therapy?

Occupational Therapy (OT) focuses on helping the child function in daily life not in abstract ways, but in the practical, everyday activities that matter most. It addresses both motor skills (how the body moves) and sensory processing (how the brain interprets input).

Eating

Managing textures, utensils, and mealtime routines.

Dressing

Tolerating fabrics, fastenings, and clothing sensations.

Writing

Building fine motor control, grip, and hand strength.

Playing

Engaging with the environment, objects, and others.

Focusing

Regulating the body enough to attend and learn.

Sensory Integration: Building Balance Through Play

One of the key approaches within OT is **Sensory Integration Therapy**. The idea is elegantly simple: if the brain learns to process sensory input more effectively, the child can respond more comfortably to the world around them.

What This Looks Like in Practice

- Activities that provide controlled sensory input
- Structured movement exercises such as swinging or jumping
- Play-based interaction tailored to the child's profile
- Gradual introduction to avoided textures or sensations

A Critical Principle

The goal is never to force discomfort. It is to understand the child's thresholds, introduce change gradually, and build tolerance over time.

Trust makes therapy progress. Without it, it becomes pressure.

Everyday Challenges Through a New Lens

When we understand sensory processing, many daily struggles suddenly become interpretable. What once felt unpredictable begins to make complete sense and when we understand, we respond very differently.

→ **Refusing certain foods**

Often linked to texture sensitivity the mouth is highly sensitive to tactile input.

→ **Avoiding crowded places**

Multiple simultaneous sensory inputs can cause genuine overload and distress.

→ **Difficulty sitting still**

The body may need movement input to feel regulated and ready to focus.

→ **Resistance to grooming**

Haircuts, nail cutting, and face washing can feel intensely uncomfortable due to touch sensitivity.

> ⓘ Understanding sensory needs does not require a diagnosis or a formal therapy programme. Awareness alone can transform daily life at home and in the classroom.

The Environment Matters and So Does Context

Small, thoughtful adjustments to the environment can make a remarkable difference. These are not special accommodations they are compassionate adaptations that support any child to feel safe and ready to learn.

At Home

- Reduce unnecessary background noise
- Choose soft, seamless clothing where possible
- Create predictable daily routines
- Allow movement breaks throughout the day

In the Classroom

- Offer a quiet corner or low-stimulation space
- Use visual schedules for predictability
- Permit sensory tools such as fidgets or cushions
- Communicate changes in routine in advance

The Reality in India

In India, awareness of sensory processing differences is still emerging. Many behaviours rooted in sensory challenges are misunderstood labelled as stubbornness, disobedience, or overreaction. Access to trained occupational therapists may also be limited outside major urban centres.

1

Build Awareness First

Understanding sensory needs can transform daily life even without access to formal therapy. Knowledge is itself a powerful intervention.

2

Advocate Within Schools

Sharing sensory frameworks with teachers and school staff helps create more supportive learning environments for children across the spectrum.

3

Seek Community Support

Parent networks, online resources, and NGO-led programmes can bridge the gap where professional services are not yet accessible.

Progress Is Subtle but Deeply Powerful

Sensory integration does not change overnight. Progress is quiet, gradual, and easy to overlook if we are only watching for dramatic shifts. But small steps are foundational each one builds the platform for the next.

1	5	1
New texture tolerated	**Extra minutes seated**	**New experience tried**
A child tries a previously refused food or fabric without distress.	Attention and regulation improving in small, measurable increments.	Attempting something unfamiliar without anxiety a significant milestone.

These may seem like small steps. But they are everything. Each one represents the nervous system learning to feel safer in the world.

A Different Way to See Behaviour

> Behaviour is not the problem. The underlying experience is. When we address the experience, behaviour often changes naturally.

Perhaps the most important shift this chapter invites is a reframe from viewing behaviour as something to correct, to viewing it as something to understand. A child who is struggling sensorially is not choosing to be difficult. They are communicating, as honestly as they can, that the world feels hard right now.

Old Lens

- The child is being difficult
- This is a discipline issue
- They are overreacting
- They need to behave better

New Lens

- The child is overwhelmed
- This is a sensory response
- Their experience is real
- They need support and co-regulation

Looking Ahead: From Regulation to Connection

With sensory and motor foundations in place, the next layer begins to emerge **social interaction and emotional understanding**. Because once the body feels regulated, the mind becomes far more available for connection.

Sensory Regulation

The body learns to feel safe and organised in the world.

Motor & Daily Skills

Practical life activities become more manageable and less stressful.

Social & Emotional Growth

A regulated nervous system opens the door to deeper connection and learning.

> The world may feel overwhelming at times. But with the right support, it can become understandable and manageable. And in that shift, a child finds not just comfort, but confidence.

Chapter 12

Social Skills & Emotional Development

Learning to connect. Learning to feel. This chapter explores the unspoken language of human interaction and how children on the autism spectrum experience, express, and gradually build emotional and social understanding. A compassionate guide for parents, caregivers, and early education professionals.

The Unspoken Language of the World

Much of human interaction is invisible not because it cannot be seen, but because it is rarely explained. A raised eyebrow. A shift in tone. A pause in conversation. These are signals: unspoken rules that guide how we connect.

Most children absorb these naturally. They learn by watching, by imitating, by experiencing. But for a child on the autism spectrum, this unspoken language is not always intuitive. What others pick up effortlessly may require deliberate effort, time, and support to understand.

Recognising this is not a failing it is the first step towards meaningful support.

Signals we rarely explain

- Raised eyebrows and facial expressions
- Shifts in tone and voice
- Pauses and conversational rhythm
- Personal space and body language
- Context-dependent responses

When the Rules Are Not Clear

Imagine entering a room where everyone seems to know the rules but no one has explained them to you. When to speak. When to wait. When to laugh. When to stop. Every interaction becomes effort. Every response becomes a decision.

In a single moment

One social situation may feel manageable there are clear cues to follow and a limited set of responses expected.

Over time

The accumulation of effort is exhausting. Processing each interaction consciously, all day, takes a significant emotional toll.

The need

Not correction· but clarity. When the rules are made visible and consistent, anxiety decreases and engagement becomes possible.

Emotion: Felt, But Not Always Expressed

One of the most misunderstood aspects of autism is emotion. There is a common belief that children on the spectrum feel less. But in reality, many feel deeply sometimes more intensely than others. The difference lies not in feeling, but in **expressing and interpreting emotion**.

Happiness felt, not shown

A child may experience genuine joy but express it differently through movement, silence, or focus rather than laughter or smiling.

Frustration without words

Frustration may be deeply felt but difficult to communicate verbally, sometimes emerging as behaviour rather than expression.

Sensing, not interpreting

A child may sense that something is emotionally significant in another person but struggle to understand what it means or how to respond.

> The gap is not in feeling it is in the bridge between feeling and sharing

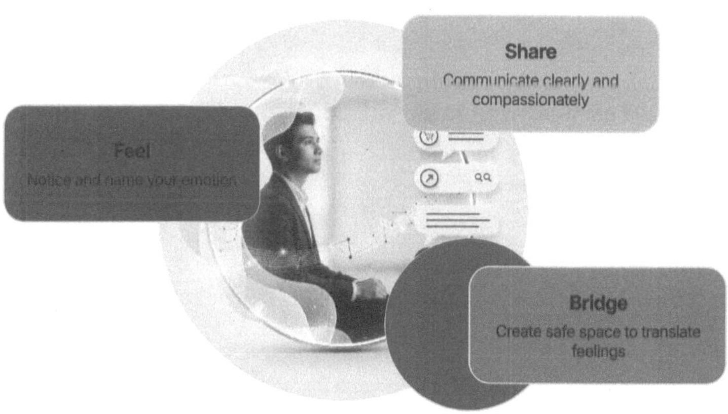

Recognising Emotions Within and Around

Understanding one's own emotions

Feelings may arrive intensely, overwhelming, and without clear labels. When a child cannot identify what they feel, they cannot begin to regulate it. Building an emotional vocabulary even a simple one is a foundational step.

- Feelings can be physical: tight chest, loud heartbeat
- Naming helps: "this is anger," "this is worry"
- Simple tools like emotion charts build awareness

Understanding others' emotions

Reading another person's emotional state requires processing multiple channels at once facial expressions, tone of voice, and context. For many children on the spectrum, this requires conscious effort and guided practice.

- Facial expressions are not always transparent
- Tone can be subtle or contradictory
- Context shapes meaning significantly

> ⓘ Both abilities self-awareness and empathy can be developed. They simply need to be explicitly supported, not assumed.

When Emotions Become Overwhelming

Without clear recognition and expression, emotions can build and when they build, they may overflow. This is often when we see meltdowns, withdrawal, or sudden behavioural shifts. Not because the child is unable to cope, but because they have not yet learned how to process what they feel.

What we see

Meltdowns, withdrawal, sudden changes in behaviour outward expressions of an internal experience that has no other outlet.

What is actually happening

Emotional build-up from unidentified or unexpressed feelings. The overflow is not defiance it is an unmet need for support.

What is needed

Not correction. Not consequences. But calm presence, consistent response, and gradual tools for emotional processing.

Teaching Social & Emotional Skills

Unlike many other aspects of development, social and emotional skills often need to be **explicitly taught** not assumed. Structure creates clarity, and clarity reduces anxiety. Over time, repeated exposure builds familiarity, and familiarity builds confidence.

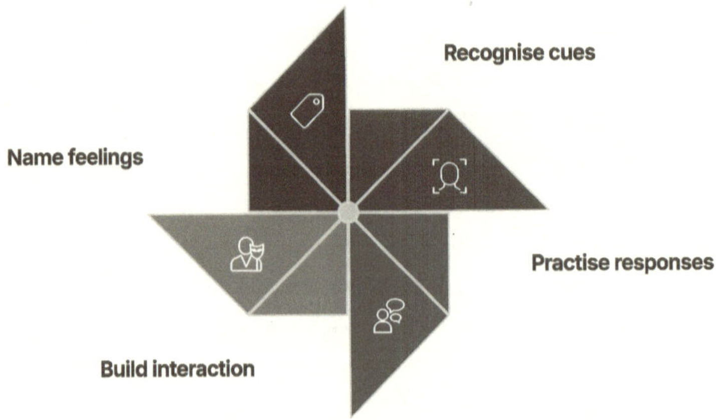

These are not small skills. They are foundational to connection and each step forward, however quiet, represents meaningful growth in a child's capacity to engage with the world around them.

Structure, Safe Relationships & the Path Forward

Learning through structure

Many children benefit from structured approaches that make the invisible visible:

- Role-playing social situations in a safe space
- Visual aids such as emotion charts and social stories
- Guided interaction in small, familiar groups

Structure reduces the cognitive load of social interaction, freeing a child to focus on connection rather than decoding.

The power of safe relationships

The most powerful space for emotional development is not a therapy room it is a relationship. A parent, caregiver, or teacher who responds consistently, accepts without judgement, and guides without pressure.

In such relationships, a child begins to trust, express, and connect. Because emotional growth requires safety above all else.

Friendship redefined

Connection may look different fewer friendships, later development, based on shared interests. This is not less. It is authentic.

Cultural context

In India, social expectations are shaped by norms around respect and participation. Patience not pressure supports real development.

Measuring growth differently

Not by comparison or timelines, but by increased comfort, reduced frustration, and greater ability to engage on one's own terms.

Connection is not taught in a single moment. It is built slowly, patiently, meaningfully. And when it begins to form, it changes not just interaction, but the entire experience of the world.

Chapter 13

Integrative Therapies

Beyond Words, Beyond Structure

Not every form of expression uses words. Not every form of learning follows a structured path. Sometimes, connection begins with something much simpler a rhythm, a colour, a movement, a moment of play. This chapter explores how creative, sensory, and experiential approaches can open new doors for children on the autism spectrum.

When Traditional Paths Feel Incomplete

What families have already built

By this stage, many families have put significant, loving effort into structured interventions speech therapy, occupational therapy, and behavioural sessions. Each is important. Each is necessary.

A quiet realisation

And yet, there are moments when something still feels incomplete. A child who participates but does not fully engage. A child who learns but does not always connect.

That quiet realisation begins to form: **maybe not everything can be taught through structure alone.**

> Perhaps what is needed is not more instruction but a different kind of space entirely.

What Are Integrative Therapies?

Integrative therapies support development through **creative, sensory, and experiential methods**. They are not replacements for structured interventions they are complements, working alongside to add depth where structure alone may not reach.

Play Therapy

Expanding the space for exploration and shared interaction through a child's natural language.

Music Therapy

Using rhythm, melody, and repetition to build connection without requiring words.

Art Therapy

Offering freedom of expression no right answers, no fixed expectations, just honest communication.

Animal-Assisted Therapy

Creating calm, non-judgemental presence that invites trust and gentle interaction.

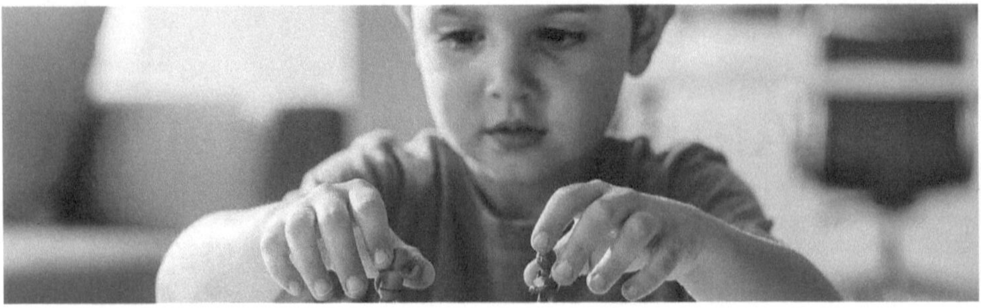

Play: The Natural Language of Childhood

For most children, play is instinctive it is how they explore, imagine, and connect. For some children on the autism spectrum, play may look different: more repetitive than imaginative, focused on objects rather than interaction.

Joining the child's world

Rather than redirecting, a play therapist enters the child's own space and builds interaction within familiar patterns.

Introducing variation slowly

Change is introduced gently, at the child's pace not imposed, but invited so curiosity can emerge naturally.

Play becomes shared

Over time, something shifts. Interaction becomes natural. Play becomes a bridge rather than a solitary experience.

Music, Art & Animal-Assisted Therapy

🎵 Music: A Different Path to Connection

Music does not demand language. It simply exists and invites response. Rhythm creates predictability, melody creates engagement, and repetition creates comfort. A beat tapped, a sound echoed and in that moment, connection begins.

> ✓ A child who struggles with verbal communication may respond to music with remarkable ease and openness.

🎨 Art: Expression Without Pressure

Art offers something rare: freedom. Through drawing, painting, or shaping, a child can communicate emotion, thought, and experience without needing words. For some, art becomes a window into their inner world a way to express what cannot yet be spoken.

🐾 Animals: Presence Without Judgement

No expectations. No complex social cues. Just presence. Interacting with animals can reduce anxiety, encourage gentle interaction, and build trust allowing confidence to grow in its own time.

Why These Approaches Matter

Integrative therapies create something that structured sessions alone cannot always provide: **space.** A space where the child is not being corrected or evaluated but simply engaged.

Emotional Expression

Children find channels to communicate what they feel, beyond the limits of spoken language.

Deeper Engagement

Learning happens more naturally, more comfortably, and more meaningfully when a child is truly present.

Genuine Connection

These therapies address the relational dimension building trust between child, adult, and the world around them.

These therapies do not replace speech or occupational therapy. They **enhance** the overall experience reaching where structure alone may not.

The Role of Joy in Development

In structured environments, the focus is often on progress goals, milestones, and outcomes. But development is not only about progress. It is also about joy.

Moments that matter

Laughter. Curiosity. Spontaneity. These are not distractions from development they are **essential to it**. When a child enjoys the process, they engage more fully. And engagement drives growth.

The reality in India

Access to integrative therapies is still growing across India, more available in urban centres than in smaller towns. Hesitation is understandable *"Is this necessary?"* but even simple adaptations at home, such as music, creative play, and sensory activities, can make a meaningful difference.

Following the Child's Lead

One of the most powerful principles in integrative therapies is simple: **follow the child**. Not every child will respond to the same approach. The role of the adult is not to decide the path in advance it is to observe and respond.

Observe

Notice what draws the child in movement, sound, texture, or creative play.

Respond

Meet the child where they are, joining their world rather than redirecting it.

Celebrate

Recognise progress that may not be measurable: increased engagement, longer moments of connection, greater comfort.

Trust

Believe that joy, expression, and connection are themselves powerful forms of growth.

> Not all growth comes from instruction. Some of it comes from expression. From connection. From joy. When we make space for that, we allow the child to show us who they are.

With therapies in place structured and integrative the next chapter turns to education: how to create learning environments that support not just academic growth, but the child as a whole.

Chapter 14

Inclusive Education vs Special Schools

A Choice, Not a Compromise. For parents of a child on the autism spectrum, choosing a school is rarely a simple decision. It is not just about education it is about **belonging**. This chapter explores both paths with honesty, compassion, and clarity, helping you make a thoughtful choice that fits your child.

The First Visit

The school looks like any other. Bright classrooms. Children in uniform. Teachers guiding lessons. From the outside, everything feels familiar and reassuring.

But inside, a quiet tension builds. As a parent, you carry questions that are rarely spoken aloud yet always present.

> *"Will my child fit here? Will they be understood? Will they be accepted?"*

These questions are not signs of doubt. They are signs of love. And they are exactly the right questions to be asking.

What Parents Are Really Searching For

→ **Safety**

A space where my child is protected

→ **Understanding**

Teachers who truly see my child

→ **Belonging**

A community where my child is valued

What Does "Inclusive" Really Mean?

The word *inclusive* appears in brochures, conversations, and policies. But inclusion is not a label it is an experience. Without genuine support, it can become symbolic: a seat in the classroom without real participation.

Present	**Supported**
The child is physically in the classroom	Structures are in place to help them thrive
Understood	**Valued**
Teachers and peers know how to respond	The child's contributions are celebrated

ⓘ True inclusion means a child is not just admitted but understood. Not just accommodated but genuinely valued as part of the community.

The Reality of Inclusive Classrooms

When Inclusion Works Well

Inclusive education at its best offers children exposure to diverse peers, meaningful social interaction, and access to the mainstream curriculum. Children learn not only academics, but also adaptability, social awareness, and confidence.

Peer Modelling

Learning from classmates naturally

Social Growth

Building real-world interaction skills

Curriculum Access

Engaging with mainstream learning

What Inclusion Requires

For inclusion to move beyond symbolism, the right foundations must be in place. Without these, a mainstream classroom can quickly become overwhelming for a child on the spectrum.

Trained Teachers

Educators equipped with autism-informed strategies

Individualised Support

Plans tailored to each child's needs

Flexible Methods

Teaching that adapts, not just accommodates

Understanding Special Schools

Special schools are designed specifically for children with developmental differences. They offer a carefully considered environment where learning is structured, paced, and personalised.

Smaller Class Sizes

More individual attention and less sensory overload

Structured Routines

Predictability that reduces anxiety and builds confidence

Specialised Teaching

Approaches matched to the child's learning style

Comfort & Clarity

An environment built around each child's needs

The Emotional Dilemma

Choosing between inclusive and special education is not just a practical decision it is an emotional one. Parents carry the weight of doubt, love, and hope all at once.

> Am I limiting my child by choosing a special school?

> Am I overwhelming my child by choosing mainstream?

There is no universally "right" answer because the right choice depends entirely on **the child**, not the system. Asking these questions means you are already thinking carefully and lovingly.

Both paths carry value. Both carry challenges. What matters most is knowing your child deeply their sensitivities, their strengths, their pace and choosing accordingly, without guilt.

It Is Not Either-Or

A FLEXIBLE APPROACH

One of the most important realisations for any family is this: education does not have to be a fixed path. A child's needs evolve and so can their schooling.

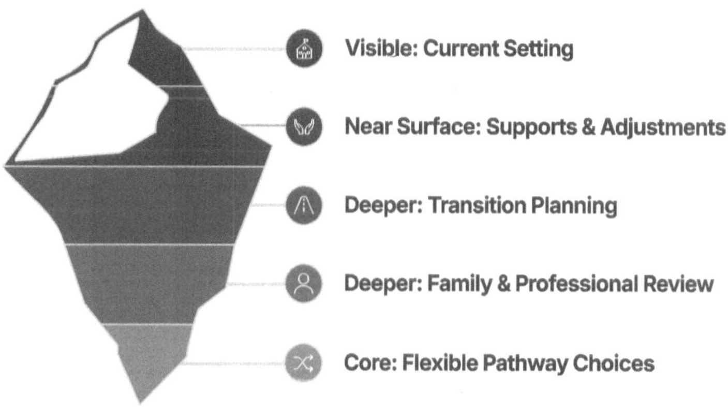

The goal is not to fit the child into a system. The goal is to find or create a system that fits the child at their current stage of development. Flexibility is not indecision. It is wisdom.

The Role of the Teacher

More than infrastructure, more than curriculum the teacher often makes the greatest difference. A single educator who truly understands, adapts, and shows patience can transform a child's entire learning experience, even within an imperfect system.

> Connection drives learning. A child who feels seen will always learn more than a child who is simply managed.

Observes

Notices the child's patterns, triggers, and strengths

Adapts

Adjusts teaching methods to suit the individual

Connects

Builds trust that unlocks genuine learning

Peer Interaction: A Hidden Layer

One of the deepest concerns parents carry is whether their child will be accepted by peers. In inclusive environments, classmates can be a powerful source of growth but also, without awareness, a source of unintentional exclusion.

✅ Peers Can Help

- Model social behaviour naturally
- Encourage interaction and friendship
- Foster a genuine sense of belonging

⚠️ Without Awareness

- Differences may be misunderstood
- Exclusion can happen unintentionally
- A child may feel isolated despite being present

🎯 The Solution

- Inclusion must extend beyond the child
- Whole-classroom awareness programmes help
- Teachers play a key role in shaping peer culture

🗒 Peer awareness programmes where all children learn about different ways of thinking and communicating can transform classroom culture for everyone.

The Reality in India

In India, inclusive education is evolving but implementation remains inconsistent across regions, schools, and communities. Parents often find themselves navigating a landscape shaped by availability, affordability, and accessibility rather than ideal suitability.

Limited Teacher Training

Many mainstream educators lack autism-specific preparation

Large Class Sizes

Individualised support is difficult at scale

Variable Quality

Both inclusive and special schools vary widely

⚠ Parents in India often make decisions with imperfect options. This is not a reflection of their care it is a reflection of systemic gaps that are gradually being addressed.

Despite these challenges, dedicated teachers, parent advocacy groups, and growing policy awareness are slowly reshaping what is possible. Many families have found excellent support and knowing where to look makes all the difference.

Beyond Academics

Education is not only about learning subjects. For a child on the autism spectrum, success may not always be measured in grades and that is not a lesser measure. It is a broader, richer one.

1st

Priority: Comfort

A child who feels safe can begin to learn

2nd

Priority: Participation

Engagement matters more than performance

3rd

Priority: Growth

Progress at any pace is still progress

Building confidence, developing independence, and creating social understanding these are outcomes worth celebrating deeply, at every stage of a child's journey.

A Choice That Evolves

What Thoughtful Decisions Look Like

01

Observe

Notice what your child responds to comfort, overwhelm, joy

02

Stay Flexible

Be willing to revisit decisions as your child grows

03

Let Go of Comparison

Your child's path is uniquely theirs

04

Adapt

The best choice today may differ from the best choice tomorrow

There is no perfect decision only a thoughtful one. And the most important thing to remember is that this decision is allowed to change. As your child grows, so does your understanding of what they need.

Letting go of comparison is one of the hardest and most freeing steps a parent can take. Not every child will follow the same path. That is not failure. That is difference. And difference, in the context of your child, is something to honour.

> The goal is not to match someone else's journey. It is to support your own child's.

Looking Ahead

Choosing the right environment is only the beginning. Once that choice is made thoughtfully, lovingly, flexibly the next question becomes: *How do we make that environment truly work for the child?*

Chapter 15 Explores

Designing autism-friendly classrooms and learning systems from sensory considerations to communication strategies

The Central Idea

Education is not about fitting into a system. It is about finding a space where a child can learn, grow, and belong

Sometimes That Space

Must be created not just chosen. And that act of creation is itself a profound form of advocacy and love

Remember: Every question you have asked, every visit you have made, every moment of doubt and hope it is all part of finding the right space for your child. You are already doing something extraordinary.

Chapter 15

Designing Autism-Friendly Classrooms

There is a moment that often goes unnoticed. A child sits in a classroom. The lesson has begun. Around them, learning is happening but for that child, something feels quietly misaligned. This chapter explores how thoughtful classroom design can transform that experience, making learning not just accessible, but genuinely possible.

The Classroom We Assume Works

A typical classroom is built on certain assumptions: that children can sit still, listen continuously, follow verbal instructions, and shift between activities with ease. For many children, these assumptions hold. For others, they don't.

When they don't, the problem is often misidentified not in the system, but in the child. Understanding this distinction is the first step toward meaningful change.

The Assumption

All children learn in broadly the same way and can adapt to a standard classroom environment without additional support.

The Reality

Neurological differences mean that standard environments can create invisible barriers barriers that are often mistaken for behavioural problems.

The Shift Needed

Moving from asking "what is wrong with this child?" to asking "what does this child need from this environment?"

When Learning Feels Overwhelming

Imagine trying to learn in a space where the noise never settles, instructions feel unclear, transitions come too quickly, and expectations are never explicitly explained. What appears as inattention may actually be overload. What appears as resistance may actually be confusion.

Appears as Inattention

May actually be **sensory overload** the child's nervous system is overwhelmed before the lesson even begins.

Appears as Resistance

May actually be **confusion** unclear instructions or unexpected changes creating genuine distress.

Appears as Disinterest

May actually be **exhaustion** the effort of navigating a difficult environment leaving no energy for learning.

The Invisible Barriers to Learning

For a child on the autism spectrum, the classroom can present multiple invisible challenges. Each may seem minor on its own but together, they create an environment that is genuinely difficult to navigate.

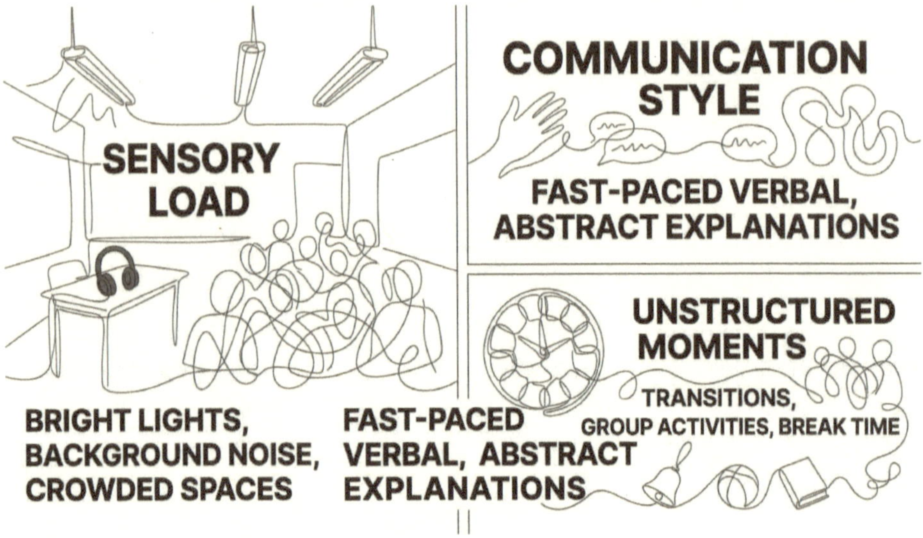

ⓘ These barriers are not always visible to teachers or other children which is why awareness and intentional design are so essential.

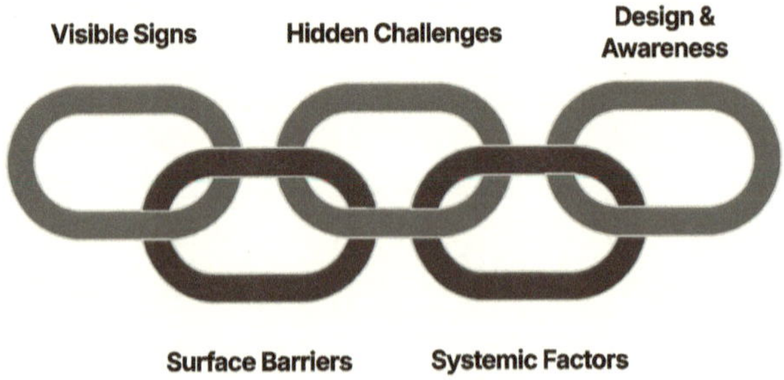

What Makes a Classroom "Autism-Friendly"?

An autism-friendly classroom is not a different building. It is a different approach one that recognises learning does not happen the same way for everyone, and adapts accordingly. It is built on three foundational principles.

Structure Creates Safety

Predictability reduces anxiety. When a child knows what will happen next, how long activities will last, and what is expected they can focus on learning rather than managing uncertainty.

Visual Support Changes Everything

Many children process visual information more effectively than verbal instruction. Schedules, step-by-step charts, and picture-based instructions create clarity that spoken words alone cannot always provide.

Simplified Communication Enables Understanding

Clear, direct, and consistent language removes the burden of interpretation not because the child cannot understand, but because clarity genuinely enables understanding.

Structure, Visuals, and Clear Communication

From This

"Finish your work and get ready for the next activity."

Fast. Layered. Implied. Difficult to process for a child who experiences language differently.

To This

1. Complete your worksheet
2. Pack your books away
3. Line up quietly at the door

Visual, sequential, and explicit. Clarity reduces confusion and confusion often drives the behaviours we struggle to understand.

Visual schedules, timers, and step-by-step instructions are not accommodations that lower expectations. They are tools that allow children to meet expectations on their own terms, in their own way.

Transitions and Movement

One of the most challenging parts of a school day is not the lesson it is the transition. From one activity to another, from classroom to playground, from structured time to unstructured time. These moments are unpredictable, and unpredictability creates stress.

1 **Advance Warning**

"Five minutes left" gives the child time to mentally prepare for what is coming next.

2 **Visual Timers**

A visible countdown removes the need to interpret verbal cues and makes time tangible.

3 **Consistent Routines**

When transitions follow a predictable pattern, they become manageable even comfortable.

> Movement is not disruption it is regulation. Allowing short movement breaks, flexible seating, and hands-on activities can improve focus, not reduce it.

Teachers, Peers, and the Path Forward

More than any tool or system, the teacher shapes the classroom experience. A teacher who understands that behaviour has meaning, that differences require adaptation, and that patience is essential creates an environment where learning becomes possible. Not perfect. But possible.

The Teacher's Role

Understanding, adapting, and responding with patience the single most powerful force in an autism-friendly classroom.

Peers as Partners

Inclusion is not passive. When guided, classmates can support, model, and create genuine opportunities for connection.

Small Changes

A quieter corner, a visual schedule, a patient explanation. These are not major interventions but they change the experience entirely.

> When the environment becomes supportive, the child begins to adapt naturally. Sometimes, the most powerful approach is not to change the child but to change the conditions around them.

A classroom is only one part of learning. In the next chapter, we explore **the role of parents in shaping learning beyond the classroom** because education does not end when school ends. Learning is not just about content. It is about conditions.

Chapter 16

The Role of Parents Where Learning Truly Begins

Learning does not begin in school. It does not begin in therapy. It begins much earlier at home, in the quiet, ordinary moments that shape everything. This chapter is for every parent who has wondered whether they are doing enough, and for every professional who supports them.

The Moments That Matter Most

Not in structured sessions. Not in planned activities. But in small, everyday moments that are easy to overlook and yet, they shape everything.

A Name Called Softly

A parent calling their child's name an act so simple, yet one of the earliest bridges of connection.

A Shared Glance

A moment of eye contact across the room carries more meaning than many structured lessons ever could.

A Hand Held in Uncertainty

When a child feels unsettled, a parent's steady hand communicates safety without a single word.

> These moments are so ordinary, they are easy to overlook. And yet, they shape everything.

When the Journey Changes

Before Diagnosis

Parenting is largely guided by instinct. Responses feel natural. Milestones arrive without needing to be tracked so closely. There is less questioning, more trusting the moment.

After Diagnosis

Something shifts. Parenting becomes more intentional more observant, more thoughtful. Every interaction begins to carry new weight. *Am I doing the right thing? Should I respond differently? Is this helping?*

The weight of responsibility increases not because parents are expected to become experts, but because they care deeply.

ⓘ Instinct does not disappear after diagnosis. It meets information. And together, they become something powerful.

From Instinct to Awareness

After a diagnosis, advice can come from everywhere therapists, doctors, schools, and other parents. Each voice brings genuine value. But when the voices are not aligned, confusion can follow.

Therapists

Offer structured strategies rooted in evidence and clinical observation.

Doctors

Provide medical context, assessments, and referrals to support services.

Schools

Share educational perspectives and progress within the learning environment.

Other Parents

Offer lived experience, empathy, and community often the most reassuring voice of all.

You Are Not Replacing the Therapist

Parents often feel pressure to "do everything" to replicate therapy at home, to constantly teach, to correct every behaviour. But home is not a therapy centre. And it should not become one.

What children need most at home

Comfort

Safety

Connection

These three things cannot be provided by a therapist. Only a parent can truly offer them and they matter more than any drill or exercise.

> The most powerful thing a parent can offer is not expert knowledge. It is consistent, loving presence.

The Power of Everyday Interaction

The most meaningful learning often happens outside formal settings in the natural rhythm of daily life. These moments offer something structured sessions cannot always replicate: safety, repetition, and genuine connection.

Mealtime Conversations

A natural space to practise turn-taking, naming, and communication without it ever feeling like a lesson.

Play

Following a child's lead in play builds trust and opens the door to genuine shared attention and joy.

Daily Routines

Predictable routines provide the structure within which a child feels safe enough to engage and explore.

> Waiting for a response, encouraging a gesture, acknowledging an attempt these simple interactions can reinforce learning more effectively than structured drills.

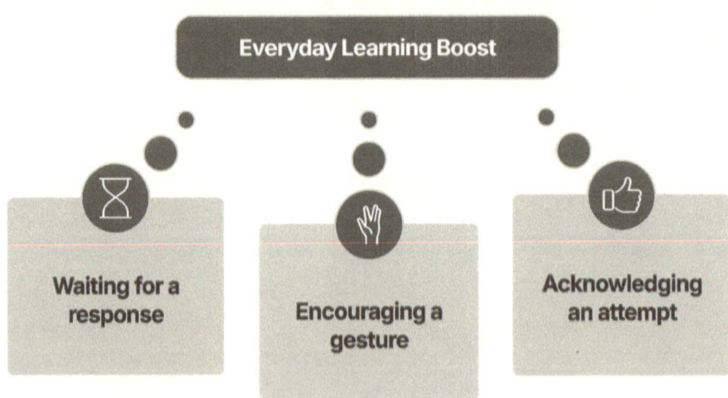

Understanding Before Responding

One of the most powerful shifts a parent can make is deceptively simple: pause before reacting. This small shift changes everything it replaces frustration with curiosity, and curiosity leads to understanding.

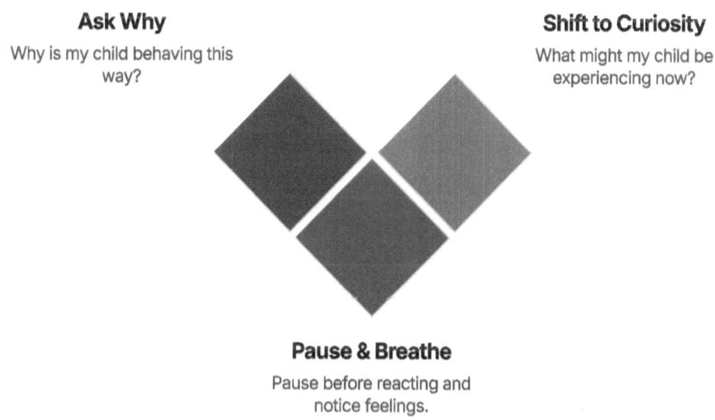

This reframing is not about dismissing difficult behaviour. It is about approaching it with compassion first which makes every subsequent response more effective and more connected.

Consistency Builds Trust

When parents respond calmly and maintain predictable routines, children begin to understand the world more clearly. Trust is the foundation on which all learning rests.

Curiosity Replaces Frustration

Asking "what is my child experiencing?" opens a window into their inner world and leads to responses that genuinely support rather than escalate.

The Emotional Foundation of Development

Beyond learning strategies and structured support, there is something even more important: emotional presence. A child who feels safe, accepted, and understood is far more likely to engage, communicate, and explore the world around them.

Emotional Security

Is not separate from development. It is the foundation of it. A regulated, connected child learns more readily than any programme alone can achieve.

Balancing Support and Space

Growth also requires space to try, to struggle, to learn. Not every moment needs correction. Sometimes, quiet observation is enough.

Redefining Success

A new attempt at communication. A calmer response. A shared moment of interaction. These are not small things. They are milestones and they deserve to be celebrated.

> There is no perfect parent. Only a present one. And presence, above all else, is what your child needs most.

The Reality in India

A Wider Circle of Care

In India, parenting often extends well beyond the immediate family. Grandparents, relatives, and community members are frequently involved in a child's upbringing and this can be a genuine strength. Shared love and attention can create a richer world for a child on the autism spectrum.

Navigating the Challenges

A wider circle can also bring complexity: differing opinions, traditional beliefs, and pressure to conform to expectations. Parents may find themselves navigating not only their child's needs but also the views of those around them. This requires clarity, patience, and sometimes, quiet strength.

ⓘ It is possible to honour family and community while also holding firm boundaries around your child's wellbeing. Both can coexist.

Caring for Yourself

In focusing entirely on the child, parents often forget themselves. But this is a long journey and sustained support can only come from sustained strength. Caring for yourself is not selfish. It is necessary.

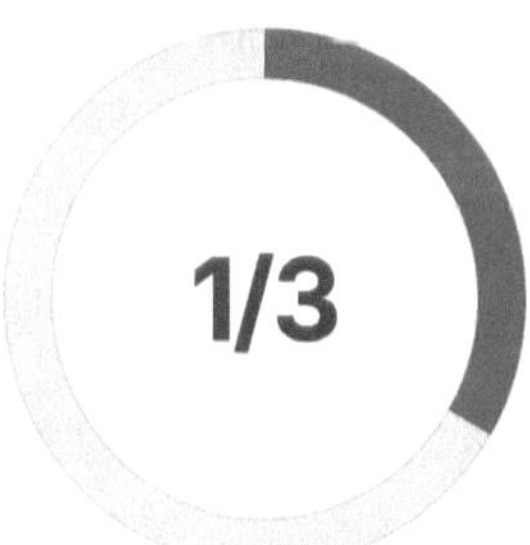

Emotional Resilience

Requires regular rest, reflection, and connection with others who understand.

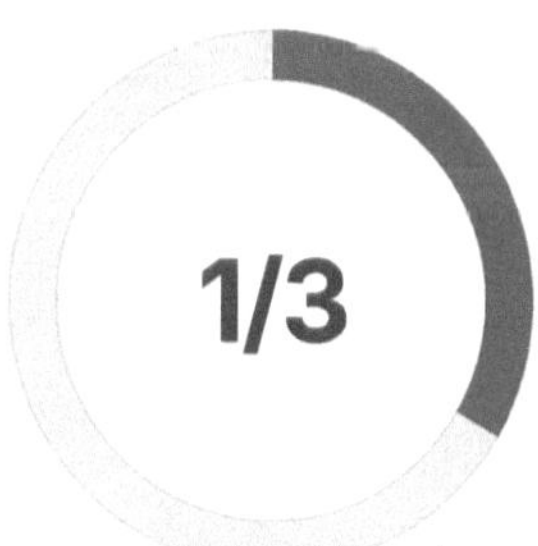

Physical Energy

Sleep, nourishment, and moments of stillness replenish the capacity to parent with patience.

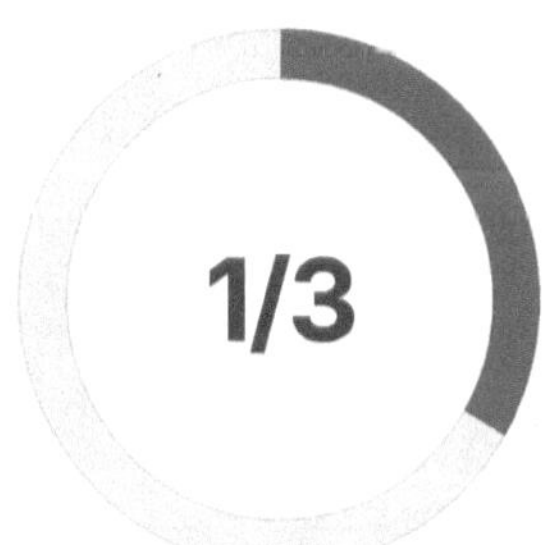

Mental Clarity

Seeking support from professionals or peer networks helps parents process, plan, and persist.

You Know Your Child

> You know your child better than anyone else. Not because you have all the answers but because you see the small changes, the subtle progress, the quiet struggles. Trust that understanding. It matters.

The Small Changes

Progress in autism rarely arrives in great leaps. It arrives in small, quiet moments that a parent is uniquely positioned to notice and celebrate.

The Subtle Progress

A slightly longer period of calm. A new sound attempted. A moment of eye contact held a little longer. Each one is real, and each one counts.

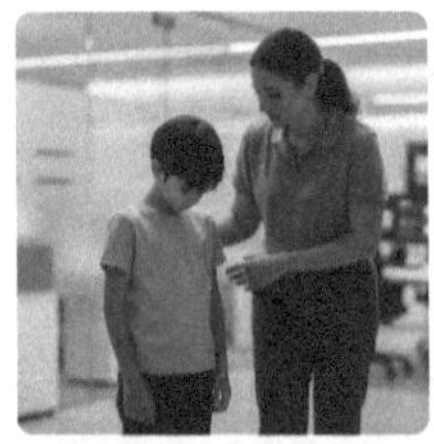

The Quiet Struggles

You see when your child is overwhelmed even before they can express it. That insight that knowing is irreplaceable in any support plan.

Looking Ahead

With the home and school working together, another dimension begins to emerge: technology. Tools that can support learning, communication, and independence are transforming what is possible for children on the autism spectrum.

1

Home

The foundation where safety, routine, and connection are built.

2

School

The bridge where skills are practised and social worlds expand.

3

Technology

The next chapter tools that amplify learning, communication, and independence.

> Parenting is not about having all the answers. It is about being present in the questions. And in that presence, a child finds not just guidance but understanding.

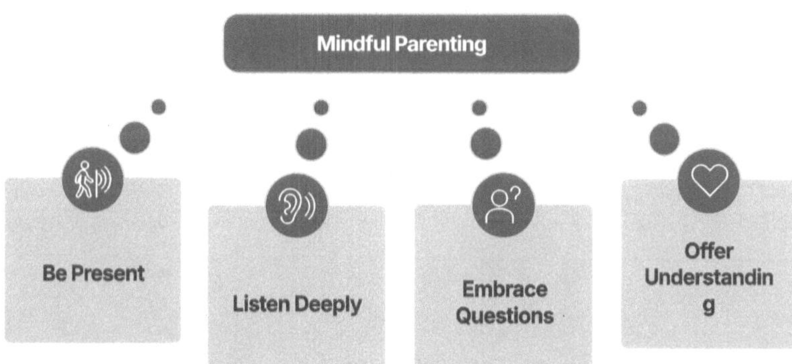

Chapter 17

Technology in Education

Extending Possibility, Not Replacing Connection For many children who learn differently, traditional classroom structures have not always been the right fit. Technology offers something powerful: adaptability. Not as a replacement for teachers or human connection, but as an extension a flexible layer of support that meets each child where they are.

When Traditional Learning Falls Short

For a child on the autism spectrum, learning is not simply about content. It is about **how** that content is presented, how quickly it is delivered, and how consistently it is reinforced. A child may struggle not because they cannot learn but because the method does not match their way of processing.

Pace

Instructions move too fast, leaving no room to pause, absorb, or revisit.

Abstraction

Concepts feel too abstract, with little visual or concrete grounding.

Environment

The classroom itself may feel overwhelming noise, unpredictability, and sensory demands all compete.

The child does not lack ability. The system lacks flexibility. And slowly, learning begins to feel difficult not because of who the child is, but because of how the environment is shaped.

A New Layer of Support

Technology introduces something transformative: **adaptability**. It is not a replacement for teachers. Not a substitute for human connection. But an extension a tool that can adjust where traditional systems often cannot.

What Technology Is

- A flexible, responsive learning tool
- An extension of human support
- A bridge between child and content

What Technology Is Not

- A replacement for teachers
- A substitute for emotional warmth
- A solution in isolation

Learning at an Individual Pace

In a traditional classroom, learning moves forward whether a child is ready or not. One of the most valuable aspects of technology is that it removes this pressure entirely. A child can move at the pace that is right for them.

1

Repeat

Revisit a lesson as many times as needed, without judgement or time pressure.

2

Pause

Take a break mid-session and return without losing progress or momentum.

3

Progress

Move forward only when the child is truly comfortable and confident.

When pressure reduces, engagement increases. Pacing is not just a convenience it is a learning strategy.

Visual Learning, Communication & Structure

Technology supports several of the most important learning needs for children on the spectrum from visual input to communication to daily structure.

Visual Learning

Animated explanations, interactive visuals, and step-by-step demonstrations make abstract concepts concrete and far easier to understand.

Communication Apps

Children who struggle with speech can select images, build sentences, and express needs clearly reducing frustration and strengthening connection.

Digital Structure

Visual schedules, task sequencing, and reminders help a child see what comes next reducing anxiety and supporting growing independence.

The Emerging Role of AI

As technology evolves, a new dimension is emerging. Artificial Intelligence has the potential to make learning not just digital but truly **responsive**. Adjusting in real time to the needs of each individual child.

Pattern Recognition

AI can identify how a child learns spotting patterns in responses, speed, and accuracy to understand individual needs.

Adaptive Content

Lessons can adjust dynamically becoming simpler, slower, or more visual depending on how the child is engaging.

Personalised Journeys

Over time, AI can map a truly individual learning path responsive to progress, difficulty, and the child's evolving strengths.

This is not the distant future. It is already beginning to emerge and for children who learn differently, the implications are profound.

The Limits of Technology And the Risk of Over-Reliance

With all its advantages, technology has important boundaries. Understanding these boundaries is not a reason to avoid technology it is a reason to use it **thoughtfully**.

What Technology Cannot Replace

- Human warmth and emotional attunement
- Real-world social interaction
- The relationship between child and carer
- Spontaneous, lived experience

The Risk of Over-Reliance

- Withdrawal from human interaction
- Reduced motivation for face-to-face communication
- Passive engagement replacing active exploration
- Screens becoming a form of avoidance

⚠ Technology should support communication not replace it. Enhance learning not isolate it. The balance is essential.

The Role of Parents & Teachers

Technology is only as effective as how it is used. Parents and teachers are the guides the humans who make thoughtful decisions about when to introduce a tool, how to integrate it meaningfully, and when to step back and let connection take over.

Introduce Intentionally

Choose tools that match the child's specific needs not simply what is popular or widely available.

Integrate Thoughtfully

Weave technology into existing routines rather than replacing them so it enhances rather than disrupts.

Step Back When Needed

Recognise when a child needs human presence more than a screen. Tools do not create outcomes. People do.

The Reality in India

In India, technology presents both remarkable opportunity and significant challenge. The gap is not only about access to devices it is about awareness, training, and structured integration into schools.

Bridging this gap requires not just access but understanding. Parents, educators, and policymakers must work together to ensure that the tools that exist reach the children who need them most.

Small Tools, Big Impact

Technology does not have to be complex to be effective. Some of the most meaningful changes come from the simplest tools already available, affordable, and easy to use. These are not advanced systems. But in the hands of a thoughtful parent or teacher, they can transform daily experience.

Visual Schedule on a Tablet

A simple picture-based schedule shows a child what comes next reducing uncertainty and helping them move through the day with greater calm.

A Communication App

Symbol-based apps allow a non-verbal child to express needs, make choices, and connect with the people around them in their own way.

A Structured Learning Game

Engaging, repetitive, and rewarding structured games build skills through play, keeping the child motivated without overwhelming them.

Technology as a Bridge

At its best, technology acts as a bridge not a destination. It connects what a child understands with what they are able to express. It bridges the gap between the structure a child needs and the flexibility that life demands.

Understanding	**Expression**
Making content accessible through visual, auditory, and interactive formats.	Opening new pathways for communication beyond speech.
Independence	**Connection**
Building routines and self-management that grow with the child.	Ultimately returning the child to stronger relationships with the world around them.

> Technology does not change who a child is. But it can change what becomes possible. And when used thoughtfully, it opens doors that were once difficult to access.

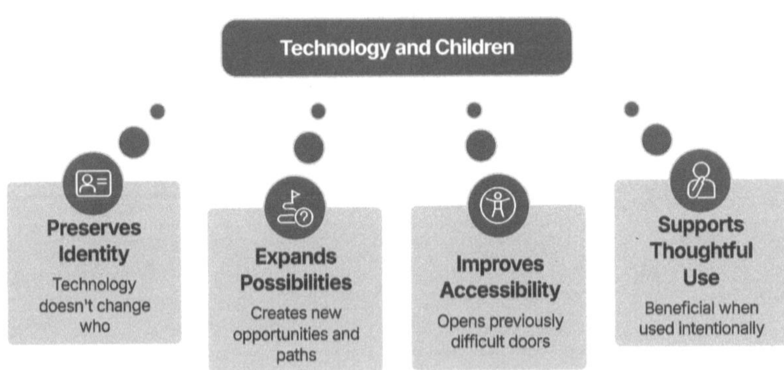

Looking Ahead Into Adolescence

With education and support systems in place, the journey begins to extend beyond childhood. Because autism is not limited to early years. It evolves. And so must the support around it.

Technology laid the foundation pacing, visuals, communication, structure. But as a child grows, new questions emerge about independence, identity, relationships, and transition into adult life.

From Tools to Transitions

The skills built through technology self-pacing, routine, expression become the foundations for navigating a wider world.

Support That Grows

Just as technology adapts to the child, support systems must adapt as the child grows remaining responsive at every stage.

Chapter 18

Parenting a Child with Autism

There is a version of parenting most people imagine a rhythm, a flow, a path that unfolds within familiar boundaries. For some parents, that path quietly changes. Not abruptly, but steadily. This chapter explores what it truly means to live that journey, every single day with love, with learning, and with extraordinary resilience.

When Parenting Becomes More Than Parenting

After a diagnosis, parenting shifts. Not in love. Not in commitment. But in **awareness.** Every moment begins to carry a new kind of weight a simple interaction becomes a learning opportunity, a small behaviour becomes a signal to interpret, and a routine becomes something to design carefully and intentionally.

Observation

Watching your child with fresh eyes noticing what they need, what overwhelms them, and what brings them comfort.

Adaptation

Adjusting your approach day by day finding what works, letting go of what doesn't, and remaining open to change.

Endless Learning

Growing alongside your child absorbing new knowledge, new strategies, and a deeper understanding of their world.

The Weight of Being "Always On"

Many parents describe a feeling they cannot easily put into words the feeling of being **constantly alert**. Watching. Anticipating. Preparing. This invisible vigilance runs quietly in the background of every outing, every transition, every new environment.

Will this environment be overwhelming?

Scanning spaces before arriving noise levels, crowds, unpredictable elements.

Will this transition be difficult?

Preparing your child and yourself for shifts in routine or setting.

Will this interaction go smoothly?

Holding your breath a little hoping, supporting, ready to step in.

This constant awareness is not visible to others. But it is very real and over time, it can become deeply tiring. You are not imagining it.

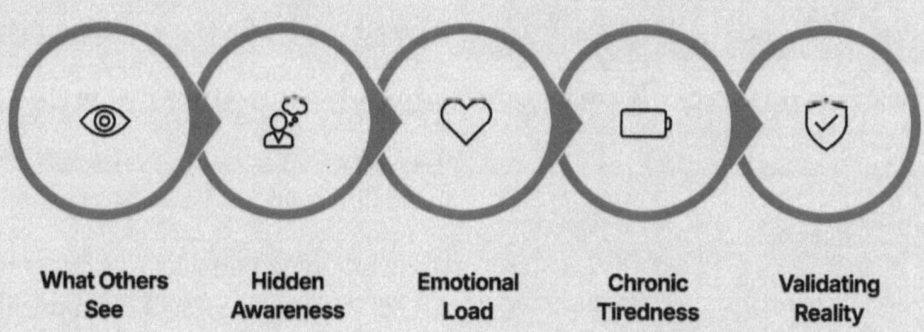

Routines: Not Restriction, But Stability

One of the first things parents learn is the profound importance of routine not as control, but as **comfort**. A predictable day creates safety, reduces anxiety, and sets clear expectations. Morning routines, mealtimes, and sleep schedules become anchors not just for the child, but for the entire family.

Morning Routines

A consistent start to the day reduces anxiety and prepares your child for what lies ahead.

Meal Times

Predictable mealtimes provide structure and reduce the stress around food and transitions.

Sleep Schedules

A calming, consistent bedtime routine supports regulation for both the child and the family.

Behaviour Through a Different Lens

The Old Question

Why is my child being difficult? Why won't they just comply? What am I doing wrong?

These questions come from a place of love but they can lead to frustration and self-blame.

The New Question

What is my child experiencing right now?

When a child refuses, reacts strongly, or withdraws suddenly, they are communicating something. This shift in perspective transforms how parents respond **frustration becomes curiosity, reaction becomes response**.

Understanding behaviour as communication is one of the most powerful reframes this journey offers.

Communication Happens Everywhere

Communication is no longer limited to words. It becomes a look, a gesture, a pattern even a behaviour. Parents begin to notice what others may not: a small signal, a subtle change, a particular sound that means something specific to their child alone.

A Look

Eye contact or the careful avoidance of it carries meaning that grows clearer over time.

A Gesture

Reaching, pointing, pulling physical communication that precedes or replaces words.

A Pattern

Repeated actions or sounds that signal emotional states comfort, distress, excitement, or need.

A Unique Language

Over time, a private language develops understood deeply by parent and child alone.

The Emotional Landscape of Parenting

Parenting in this context is not just practical it is **deeply emotional**. And the full range of those emotions deserves to be named and honoured. These feelings do not cancel each other out. They coexist, sometimes within the same hour of the same day.

Moments of Light

- Pride in your child's unique achievements
- Joy in small, unexpected connections
- Deep love that grows through challenge
- Delight in moments of pure play

Moments of Weight

- Doubt about whether you are doing enough
- Fatigue from the relentless pace of care
- Quiet worry about the future
- Loneliness that is hard to explain to others

> Both sets of feelings are valid. Both are part of the journey. Feeling all of this does not mean you are struggling it means you are fully present.

The Invisible Strength

What often goes unrecognised is the **remarkable resilience** parents build not suddenly, but gradually. Strength does not arrive all at once. It is built in everyday moments, through learning, advocating, adapting, and showing up again and again.

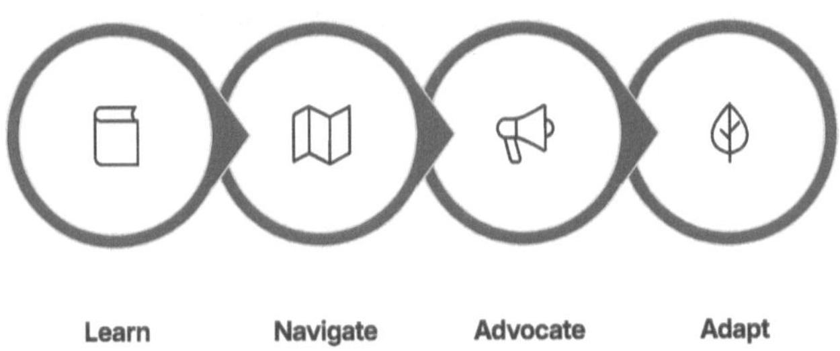

This resilience is rarely visible from the outside but it is one of the most extraordinary things a parent can develop. Every day you continue, you are building it.

The Role of the Family

Parenting does not happen in isolation. In many households especially across India family plays a central and meaningful role. Grandparents, relatives, and extended support systems can be a profound source of strength. Yet this same closeness can bring its own complexity.

Sources of Strength

- Shared care and practical support
- Emotional presence and belonging
- Cultural continuity and connection

Common Challenges

- Differing beliefs about autism
- Lack of awareness or outdated ideas
- Pressure to conform to expectations

Navigating this terrain requires both **patience and clarity** gently educating loved ones whilst holding firm in your understanding of your child's needs.

Letting Go of Comparison

One of the most difficult and liberating steps in this journey is learning to **let go of comparison.** Not every child will follow the same timeline, reach milestones in the same way, or fit into expected patterns and that is not failure. It is difference. And difference deserves its own celebration.

Release the Timeline

Your child's milestones are real and meaningful even when they arrive differently or later than expected.

Quieten External Voices

Well-meaning comparisons from others can sting. It is all right to protect your peace by setting gentle boundaries.

Grow Into Acceptance

Acceptance is not giving up it is choosing to see your child clearly and love them completely.

Finding Moments of Joy

Amid routines, therapy, and structure, it is easy to lose sight of something beautifully simple: **joy**. A shared laugh. A playful moment. A connection made without any expectation attached to it. These moments matter deeply not as a reward for hard work, but as the heart of the journey itself.

> "This journey is not only about effort. It is also about experience shared, felt, and remembered together."

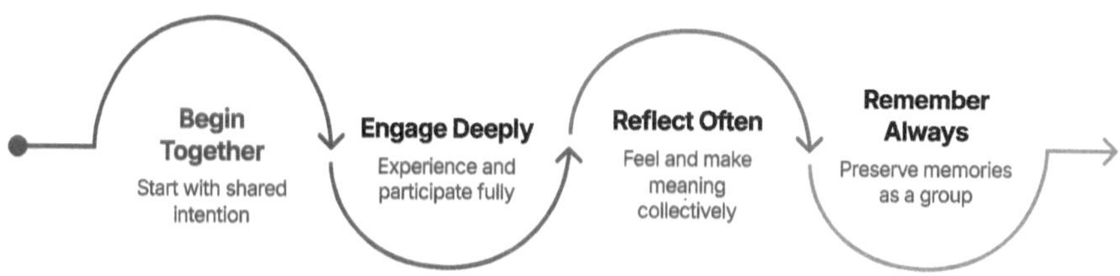

🎈 Play Without Purpose

Follow your child's lead in play no goals, no outcomes, just presence.

😄 Shared Laughter

Notice what makes your child light up and let it make you light up too.

✨ Small Celebrations

Mark the small wins with genuine delight they are not small at all.

Caring for the Caregiver

One of the most overlooked truths in this journey is this: **parents need support too.** Not because they are weak but because the journey is genuinely demanding. Sustained care requires sustained strength. And that strength cannot be drawn from an empty well.

What Self-Care Actually Looks Like

- Asking for help without guilt
- Connecting with other parents who understand
- Making space for your own emotions not just your child's
- Seeking professional support when needed
- Protecting even small pockets of rest and restoration

A Gentle Reminder

Taking care of yourself is not selfish. It is one of the most important things you can do for your child.

You cannot pour from an empty cup and you deserve to be filled too.

Redefining Parenting Itself

Over time, something deeper and quieter changes. Parenting is no longer measured against a predefined path or a checklist of expected milestones. It becomes something richer something more human.

From Following a Script

Letting go of the version of parenting that was imagined before the one that followed predictable steps and familiar markers.

To Writing Your Own

Stepping into a version of parenting defined by deep understanding, flexible adaptation, and wholehearted support of a unique journey.

And in this process, something unexpected happens **parents themselves evolve**. The journey that asks so much of you also gives something back a depth of understanding, a breadth of compassion, and a capacity for love that continues to grow.

Chapter 19

Sibling & Family Dynamics

In every family, there are stories that are visible appointments, therapies, school decisions. And then there are quieter dynamics that evolve beneath the surface, often unspoken, often unnoticed. This chapter explores those hidden relationships: the siblings who watch, adapt, and love in ways we sometimes forget to acknowledge. Understanding these dynamics is one of the most compassionate things a family can do.

e Child Who Is Watching

In many homes, there is another child watching, listening, and understanding far more than we might realise. Long before we find the right words to explain, siblings are already forming their own sense of the world around them.

They notice the extra appointments, the adjustments in daily routines, the moments of tension even when nothing is said aloud. And quietly, over time, they begin to make meaning of it all.

> ⓘ Children are perceptive. What is left unsaid is often felt most deeply.

What Siblings Often Observe

- The extra attention their sibling receives
- Adjustments made in daily family life
- Moments of parental stress, even when unspoken
- Changes in plans and routines
- How others outside the family react

Questions That Are Not Always Asked

Siblings often carry questions they may not know how to voice. These are not questions born of resentment they are born of curiosity, and sometimes confusion.

> **"Why is my brother different?"**
>
> A natural search for understanding not judgment.

> **"Why does my sister get more attention?"**
>
> A need for reassurance, not a complaint.

> **"Did I do something wrong?"**
>
> A child making sense of change the only way they can.

When these questions are left unaddressed, they do not disappear they quietly grow. Creating space for children to ask, wonder, and be heard is one of the most meaningful gifts a parent can give.

The Balance of Attention

One of the most delicate challenges for parents is balance. A child with autism may genuinely require more time, more structure, and more focused attention and that is entirely understandable. But this shift in the family dynamic can leave siblings feeling overlooked, not because they are loved less, but because demands are simply uneven.

What a child with autism may need

- More structured time and routines
- Dedicated therapeutic support
- Greater parental attention day-to-day

How siblings may feel as a result

- Secondary or overlooked
- Less prioritised or celebrated
- Uncertain about their place in the family

Recognising the imbalance is not a failure it is the first step towards addressing it with care.

The Emotional Spectrum of Siblings

Siblings of children with autism experience a remarkably wide range of emotions often all at once. Love and frustration. Pride and confusion. Protectiveness and exhaustion. All of these feelings are completely valid, and all of them deserve space.

Love & Protectiveness

Many siblings become fierce advocates defending their brother or sister without hesitation in public.

Confusion & Uncertainty

Understanding autism takes time. Siblings may feel unsure about what it means for their family's future.

Pride & Maturity

Watching a sibling grow and achieve, however differently, often fills children with a quiet, deep pride.

Frustration in Private

What is defended in public may be grieved in private. Both are real, and both are okay.

Growing Up Faster and the Weight That Comes With It

In many families, siblings develop a certain maturity early. They learn patience, adaptability, and a sense of responsibility that children their age may not yet carry. They step in to help, to explain, to support.

And while these qualities are truly remarkable a gift, in many ways they also come with weight. Childhood, in some ways, becomes different for them too. It is important to honour both the strength *and* the sacrifice that often goes unrecognised.

→ **Patience**

Learning to wait, adapt, and respond calmly.

→ **Responsibility**

Stepping in naturally, often without being asked.

→ **Empathy**

A deep, lived understanding of difference and acceptance.

The Importance of Open Conversations

Silence, however well-intentioned, can create distance. Children are remarkably perceptive they sense tension, notice change, and fill in the gaps with their own imagination. Open, honest, age-appropriate conversation is far more reassuring than protective silence.

These do not need to be formal family discussions. Often the most powerful conversations happen naturally during a car journey, at bedtime, over a meal. What matters most is that siblings feel heard, not judged, and that their feelings are welcomed rather than managed.

Giving Each Child Their Own Space

Every child needs to feel that they are seen as an individual not simply as part of the family's larger story. Small, intentional efforts can make an enormous difference in reassuring a sibling that they matter just as much.

One-on-One Time

Even brief, undivided attention sends a powerful message of love and priority.

Celebrate Their Achievements

Notice their milestones. Cheer their efforts. Make their wins feel significant.

Listen Without Distraction

Put the phone down. Make eye contact. Let them know this moment is theirs.

> *"You matter too."* The quiet message every sibling needs to hear, again and again.

The Role of Extended Family

Family dynamics extend well beyond the immediate household. In many families particularly across India grandparents, aunts, uncles, and extended relatives play a significant role in daily life and decision-making.

Extended family members can be a wonderful source of support. But they may also misunderstand the condition, make unhelpful comparisons between children, or offer advice rooted in limited awareness. This tension is rarely intentional it stems from a lack of understanding, not a lack of love.

⚠ Comparisons between siblings however casually made can cause lasting emotional impact. Gentle, consistent education within the family matters.

They May Offer

- Practical help and childcare
- Emotional support
- A sense of community

They May Also

- Misunderstand autism
- Make unhelpful comparisons
- Give advice based on outdated views

Siblings as Lifelong Support Systems

The sibling relationship is one of the longest relationships a person will ever have. As children grow into adulthood, siblings often become among the most important support systems not because they were told to be, but because the bond was nurtured over years of shared experience.

1. **Childhood**

   Growing up together, learning patience and empathy through everyday life.

2. **Adolescence**

   Navigating identity and belonging while carrying a unique family experience.

3. **Early Adulthood**

   Offering companionship, guidance, and beginning to share responsibility.

4. **Long-Term**

   Becoming a deeply meaningful, lifelong source of support and connection.

Letting Siblings Be Children

A gentle reminder

Amid all the awareness, responsibility, and maturity siblings are still children. They are still learning. They are still growing.

Support should never become burden. Responsibility should never replace play.

It is a delicate balance to hold: honouring the maturity a sibling may show, whilst also fiercely protecting their right to simply be a child. They need freedom to play, to be silly, to have their own friendships and passions entirely separate from the family's wider journey.

- Allow them time that is theirs alone
- Resist placing adult worries on young shoulders
- Celebrate the things that make them uniquely *them*
- Let joy and lightness exist alongside the serious moments

The Strength Hidden in Family Bonds

Families that navigate this journey together often discover something quietly remarkable a depth of understanding, a resilience, and an emotional closeness that is not easily visible, but is deeply, profoundly felt.

Deeper Understanding

Living alongside difference teaches empathy in ways that no classroom ever could.

Stronger Connection

Families that communicate openly build bonds that are rooted in honesty and trust.

Shared Resilience

Navigating challenges together creates a collective strength that sustains every member.

> *"Not all relationships are shaped by words. Some are shaped by experience, by adjustment, by quiet understanding. And within a family, those unseen bonds often become the strongest of all."*

Chapter 20

Social Inclusion & Public Awareness

There are moments that stay with parents a look from a stranger, a comment that lands sharply, a situation that becomes unexpectedly difficult. This chapter explores what it truly means to move beyond tolerance and build a world where every child belongs not just in policy, but in everyday life.

The World Outside the Home

Inside the Home

Patterns are known. Responses are familiar. Differences are understood and accepted. The home is a place of safety and predictability.

Outside the Home

The rules are unspoken. Expectations are rigid. Awareness is limited. A simple visit to a park, a store, or a gathering can suddenly feel uncertain not because of your child, but because the world has not yet caught up.

For many families, this gap between the home environment and the outside world is one of the most challenging realities of daily life.

When Difference Is Misunderstood

Autism is not always visible. There are no obvious markers which means behaviour is often interpreted, but rarely understood.

What Others May See

Disobedient

A child not following instructions

Rude

A child avoiding interaction

Poorly managed

A child reacting intensely

What Is Actually Happening

Sensory overload

The environment is overwhelming

Communication differences

Response looks different, not absent

Genuine need

Not defiance a real, unmet need

Not because people are unkind but because they are unaware. Awareness is where change begins.

The Weight of Public Judgement

For parents, the hardest moments are often not about the child's behaviour itself but about the reactions of the world around them. The stares. The whispers. The unsolicited advice that cuts deep.

> "Control your child." "Why is he behaving like this?"

These words spoken or unspoken — stay. And over time, they can lead to something profound: **avoidance**. Parents begin to limit outings, choose quieter spaces, and withdraw from social situations. Not out of choice but out of protection.

→ **Judgement from others**

Stares, whispers, and unsolicited comments in public spaces

→ **Emotional accumulation**

Each experience adds to an invisible weight carried by families

→ **Social withdrawal**

Families retreat not by choice, but as a form of self-protection

Inclusion Is Not Just Access

Inclusion is often misunderstood as *presence* simply allowing a child into a space. But a child may be physically present and yet emotionally excluded. True inclusion is about **experience**, not just entry.

Understanding

Recognising that behaviour has a reason and seeking to learn what that reason is

Acceptance

Not expecting sameness or conformity allowing individuals to exist as they truly are

Adaptation

Adjusting environments and expectations to meet diverse needs, not the other way around

Without all three elements, inclusion remains incomplete a door open in name only.

The Power of Small Interactions

Inclusion is not built through large policies alone. It is built in the quiet, everyday moments that most people never notice but that families never forget.

The Educator

A teacher who takes a moment to explain differences to a class creating a culture of curiosity rather than judgement

The Parent

A parent who encourages their child to be kind to someone who seems different planting seeds of empathy early

The Stranger

Someone who chooses patience over reaction in a difficult moment and changes the entire experience for a family

Cultural Context: Navigating Awareness in India

In India, awareness of autism is growing but unevenly. In urban areas, conversations are increasing. In many other spaces, silence remains. Families often navigate not just the challenges of autism itself, but the additional weight of social stigma and cultural expectation.

Key challenges include:

- Stigma around developmental differences and fear of labelling
- Limited public understanding of what autism is and how it presents
- Hesitation to speak openly, even among families with strong internal acceptance
- Uneven access to information between urban and rural communities

Urban Areas

Growing conversation and increasing community support networks

Rural Areas

Silence still predominates awareness campaigns are urgently needed

Families

Often navigating both personal acceptance and external judgement simultaneously

From Awareness to Belonging

Awareness is the first step but it is not the final one. The journey from a world that merely tolerates difference to one that genuinely embraces it moves through several stages. Each step matters.

This progression does not happen overnight but it begins with intention. Every family that steps into a public space, every educator who takes a moment to explain, every community that chooses flexibility over rigidity each one moves the needle forward.

> **Looking ahead:** Beyond society, there is another system families must navigate healthcare. In the next chapter, we explore access, affordability, and the support structures that make a difference. 👉 **Navigating Healthcare & Support Systems**

> Inclusion is not about changing the individual. It is about expanding the world around them. And when that world begins to understand, belonging becomes possible.

Chapter 21

Navigating Healthcare & Support Systems

There is a moment many parents remember clearly. Not the diagnosis. Not the first therapy. But what comes after the realisation that understanding the condition was only the beginning. Navigating the system is a journey in itself, and this chapter is here to walk alongside you through it.

The Search for Help

After diagnosis, one question becomes urgent: *Where do we go from here?* The answers are not always clear. Families begin to search for therapists, clinics, specialists, and schools each offering a piece of support, but rarely a complete path forward.

Therapists

Speech, occupational, and behavioural therapists form the core of early intervention support.

Clinics & Specialists

Medical professionals and developmental specialists provide assessments and ongoing guidance.

Schools & Educators

Finding the right educational environment is one of the most significant decisions a family faces.

A System That Exists But Not Together

At first glance, the system appears to exist. Speech therapists, occupational therapists, behavioural specialists, and medical professionals are all out there. But these elements often function in isolation disconnected and uncoordinated.

Parents become the link between them. Carrying information. Making decisions. Trying to create coherence where none exists. It is an exhausting and often invisible role.

> You did not train for this role but you are showing up for it every single day. That matters enormously.

Becoming the Coordinator

Over time, parents take on a role they never planned for: **Coordinator.** They manage appointments, therapy schedules, progress tracking, and communication between professionals all while still being caregivers, parents, and emotional anchors. It is a role that requires both strength and endurance.

Managing Appointments

Juggling multiple specialists, clinics, and school meetings whilst ensuring nothing falls through the cracks.

Therapy Scheduling

Coordinating session timings, transport, and the child's energy levels across the week.

Progress Tracking

Documenting milestones, setbacks, and responses to different interventions for each professional.

Professional Communication

Relaying information between therapists, doctors, and educators who rarely speak directly to one another.

The Challenge of Access & Cost

Unequal Access

Access is not equal. In many places, especially in India, families face limited availability of trained professionals, long waiting periods, and significant geographic constraints. Urban centres may offer options; smaller towns often do not meaning families must travel long distances, relocate temporarily, or compromise on support.

The Cost of Care

Therapy sessions, assessments, and specialised education accumulate significant expense over time. For many families, this becomes a burden not just financially, but emotionally. Decisions begin to involve difficult trade-offs: *What can we afford? What do we prioritise?* These are questions no parent should carry alone.

ⓘ If you are facing financial strain, reach out to local NGOs, government disability schemes, or parent networks many families have found unexpected support through community connections.

Insurance, Policy & The Information Gap

In many systems, insurance coverage is limited it may not fully support developmental therapies, long-term interventions, or specialised services. Government policies exist, but access can be complex, requiring documentation, certification, and eligibility navigation that is far from straightforward.

Insurance Gaps

Many developmental therapies fall outside standard policy coverage, leaving families to fund critical support out of pocket.

Policy Complexity

Government schemes exist but navigating eligibility, paperwork, and certification processes demands time and persistence.

The Information Gap

The biggest challenge is often not the absence of services it is the absence of clear information. Many families rely on word of mouth, online searches, and informal networks, creating deep inconsistency in who finds help early.

What Families Truly Need

What families need is not more services in isolation it is **connected services**. A system where professionals communicate, plans are aligned, and progress is shared. An ecosystem, not a collection of disconnected interventions.

1

Integrated Care

Professionals who communicate and coordinate with one another around a shared plan for the child.

2

Human Support

Counselling, community spaces, and peer networks where parents can ask questions and feel understood.

3

NGO Bridges

Community organisations that provide awareness, training, and affordable services bridging the gap between what exists and what is truly accessible.

The Emotional Journey and What Lies Ahead

Navigating the system is not just logistical it is deeply emotional. Every decision carries weight. Every delay creates concern. Every success brings relief. And through it all, parents continue, because the goal remains constant: **support the child.**

> Families should not have to fight the system to find support. The system should support the families. And when that happens, the journey becomes not easier but more guided.

Small Wins Matter

A good therapist found. A supportive school identified. A routine that works. These moments bring stability and deserve to be celebrated.

Systems Must Evolve

The responsibility does not lie only with families. Support must become more accessible, more affordable, and more integrated structured, not dependent on persistence alone.

Looking Ahead

Next, we move into a broader phase of life adolescence, identity, and growth. Chapter 22: *Transition to Teenage Years.*

Chapter 22
Transition to Teenage Years

There is a phase in every child's life when change becomes visible not just in height or voice but in something deeper. A quiet shift from childhood into something more complex. For parents of children on the autism spectrum, understanding this transition can make all the difference in offering the right support at the right time.

When Childhood Begins to Fade

The routines remain. The environment may stay the same. But something within the child begins to change; questions emerge, reactions evolve, and emotions deepen. For parents, there is a quiet realization: *this is a new phase.*

What Parents Notice

- Shifts in mood or behavior
- New questions about themselves
- Different responses to familiar routines
- Growing self-awareness

What This Means

Adolescence doesn't announce itself. It arrives gradually sometimes in small ways that are easy to miss. Recognizing these early signs gives families time to prepare, adjust, and respond with patience rather than surprise.

> This phase is not a problem to solve. It is a passage to navigate together.

Growth That Does Not Wait

Adolescence arrives whether we feel ready or not. The body changes naturally and gradually but emotional and social readiness may not follow at the same pace. This creates a gap that parents need to understand and gently bridge.

Physical Changes

New sensations in the body that can feel unfamiliar, surprising, or even distressing without proper preparation.

Emotional Shifts

Feelings that arrive more intensely, more suddenly, and may be harder to name or express than before.

Social Awareness

An increasing sense of others their reactions, expectations, and how one fits (or doesn't fit) into the social world.

A child may experience all of these changes without fully understanding what is happening. That's why explanation matters early, clearly, and often.

The Challenge of Explaining Change

For many parents, this phase introduces conversations that feel unfamiliar or uncomfortable. But these conversations are essential and they require a different approach: clear, direct, and without assumption. Indirect communication may not land the way you intend.

Body Changes

Explain what is happening physically calmly, factually, and without euphemism. Use correct terms and give time for questions.

Personal Hygiene

Establish new routines with clear steps. Hygiene needs change during adolescence and must be taught explicitly, not assumed.

Privacy & Boundaries

Help your child understand personal privacy their own and others'. Clear language about boundaries creates both safety and respect.

When Emotions Become More Intense

Adolescence is often described as an emotional phase. For individuals on the autism spectrum, this intensity can feel amplified feelings may appear suddenly, last longer, and be harder to interpret or express.

How It May Look

→ **Withdrawal** pulling back from family, routines, or social situations

→ **Irritation** reacting more strongly to everyday frustrations

→ **Behavioral changes** shifts that may seem sudden or hard to explain

What's Really Happening

Beneath these responses lies something important: **the effort to process.** These are not failures of behavior they are signs of a nervous system working hard to manage unfamiliar internal experiences.

> Behavior is communication. When words aren't available, the body speaks instead.

Awareness of Difference and New Questions

In earlier years, differences may not be fully recognized. But during adolescence, awareness increases. A young person begins to notice social differences, learning challenges, and how peers react to them. This awareness can bring questions spoken or unspoken.

> Why am I different?

> Why is this harder for me?

> Do I belong here?

These questions may not always be spoken aloud but they are felt deeply. Parents who create space for these conversations, without rushing to fix or reassure, give their child something invaluable: the experience of being heard.

> ⓘ You don't need to have all the answers. Being present and honest "I don't know, but we can figure it out together" is enough.

The Social World Becomes More Complex

Friendships change during adolescence. They become less structured, more nuanced, and more dependent on unspoken social rules. For someone who already finds social interaction challenging, this shift can feel overwhelming situations that once felt manageable may now feel unpredictable.

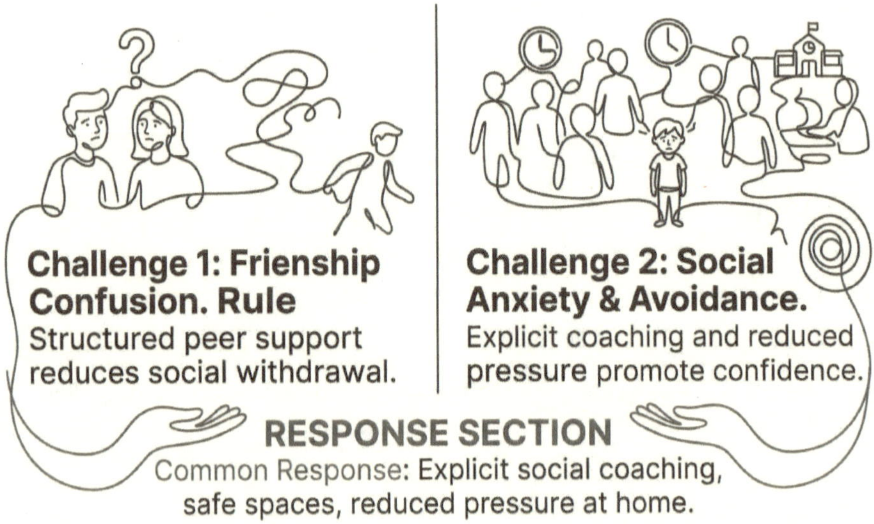

Withdrawal in these moments is not avoidance it is a coping strategy. Reducing exposure to uncertainty, misunderstanding, and social pressure is a reasonable response to an overwhelming environment. The goal isn't to eliminate withdrawal, but to build skills that gradually make the social world feel safer.

Supporting Identity, Independence & Safety

THE THREE PILLARS OF ADOLESCENT SUPPORT

Safety & Awareness

Teach personal boundaries, safe vs. unsafe situations, and appropriate social behavior explicitly, not by assumption. Clarity creates protection.

Gradual Independence

Introduce personal care, daily responsibilities, and simple decision-making step by step. Skills practiced early begin to take real shape during this phase.

Identity Formation

Help your child explore who they are their strengths, interests, and values. This process may take longer, and that's okay. What matters is consistent encouragement along the way.

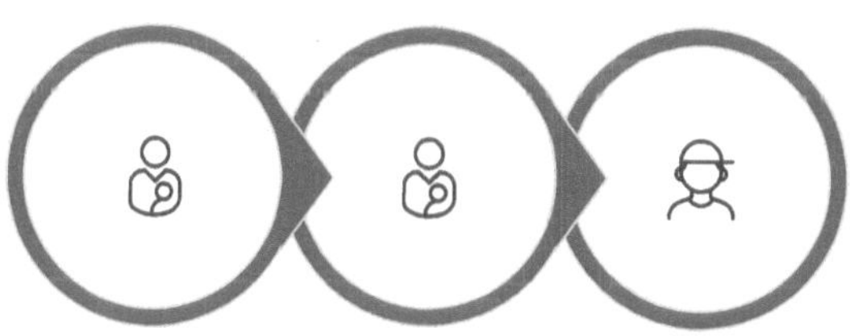

Parent Directs **Parent Supports** **Child Leads**

The parenting role shifts during adolescence from directing to supporting, from managing to enabling. This transition requires trust, and that trust is built one small step at a time.

A Phase of Transition, Not Completion

Adolescence is not the end of development it is a passage. Some skills may still be forming. Some understanding may still be evolving. That is not a delay. It is a different pace, and a pace that deserves respect.

> Growing up is not about becoming someone else. It is about becoming more aware, more capable, more confident in one's own way.

Chapter 23

Skills for Independence

Learning to Live, One Step at a Time

There is a moment when the focus begins to shift not away from learning, but beyond it. From *what is my child learning?* to *how will my child live?* This chapter explores the everyday skills, emotional realities, and gradual transitions that shape a life of confidence and autonomy.

The Quiet Question Behind Every Decision

For years, the journey has been carefully guided therapies, schooling, routines. Each step supported, each milestone celebrated. But slowly, another question begins to take shape:

> *Will my child be able to manage daily life?*

Not in the distant future. But in everyday reality. This question does not arrive with an answer. It arrives as an invitation to look ahead with intention, and to begin preparing for a life that unfolds beyond the therapy room and the classroom.

> Independence is not a destination. It is a direction built one ordinary day at a time.

From Therapies

Structured support and guided learning

To Daily Life

Applied skills and real-world confidence

Toward Autonomy

Living with dignity and self-direction

Independence Is Not What We Imagine

When people speak of independence, they often imagine complete self-sufficiency living alone, managing everything without help. But independence is not absolute. It is **layered**.

For Some

Managing personal care, following a routine, and communicating needs clearly

For Others

Extending further financial awareness, social navigation, community participation

Both Are Valid

Independence is not defined by comparison. It is defined by **capability**.

The Small Skills That Shape Life

Independence is built through everyday actions simple, repetitive, and essential. These tasks may seem ordinary, but they form the foundation of autonomy. They are the building blocks that allow a person to move through the world with agency and confidence.

Personal Care

Brushing teeth, bathing, and grooming the daily rituals of self-respect

Getting Dressed

Selecting clothes, managing fasteners, dressing with growing independence

Eating Independently

Using utensils, managing portions, and building mealtime confidence

Packing & Organizing

Following a checklist, preparing bags, owning their own belongings

Structure Creates Confidence

Why Structure Works

Just as in earlier stages, structure plays a key role in building independence. Visual schedules, checklists, and routine-based learning give children a framework to act within and over time, what begins as guided activity becomes independent action.

- Clarity about what happens next
- Predictability that reduces anxiety
- A sense of control and ownership

Learning That Requires Patience

For many individuals on the spectrum, daily skills are not absorbed automatically. They require clear instruction, step-by-step guidance, and repetition over time. A task may need to be broken down not once, but many times.

Progress may be gradual. But it is real. And it accumulates into something remarkable.

Visual supports picture-based schedules, color-coded checklists, first-then boards — transform abstract expectations into clear, actionable steps that build genuine competence.

Decision-Making & Responsibility

Independence is not only about completing tasks it is about making choices. What to wear. What to eat. What to do next. And with choice comes responsibility. These two pillars grow together, each reinforcing the other.

1

Start Small

Offer limited options two choices, not ten to make decisions feel manageable

2

Build Familiarity

Repeat similar choices until confidence grows and hesitation fades

3

Expand Gradually

Introduce more complex decisions as readiness develops over time

Growing Responsibility

Simple responsibilities putting things back in place, completing small tasks, following daily routines build something deeper than compliance. They build **ownership, accountability, and confidence.**

→ Completing a task they started

→ Returning items to their place

→ Following a routine without prompting

The Emotional Side of Independence

Independence is not only practical. It carries deep emotional weight for the child, and for the parent. Growth in autonomy brings both joy and challenge in equal measure.

What It Brings

- A sense of achievement and pride
- Increased confidence in daily life
- Greater self-awareness and identity

What It Can Also Bring

- Anxiety about new situations
- Fear of making mistakes
- Uncertainty in unfamiliar territory

The Role of Mistakes

Not every mistake needs to be avoided. Some need to be experienced. Space to try, to struggle, and to learn is where real independence takes root.

Support remains important even as autonomy grows. The goal is not to remove the safety net, but to gradually widen the space in which the child moves freely.

The Parent's Evolving Role

At this stage, parenting shifts once more. The transition is not sudden it unfolds gradually, and it requires trust. Trust in the process, and trust in the child. This balance between support and freedom is perhaps the most nuanced skill a caregiver can develop.

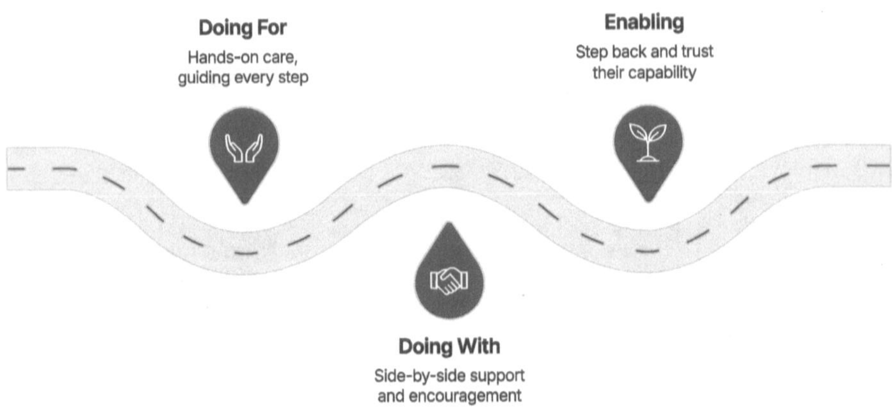

⚠ Too much support can limit growth. The instinct to protect is natural but independence requires space to try and even to stumble.

In India, strong family structures are a gift but conscious effort is needed to encourage independence when the child is truly capable, even out of care.

> **Independence is not about doing everything alone. It is about living with confidence, dignity, and the ability to navigate the world and every small step taken today moves closer to that reality.**

Chapter 24

Employment & Careers

Finding a Place in the World a quiet question that carries immense weight: *What will my child do in life?* Not just in terms of skills learned, but in terms of purpose. This chapter explores how individuals on the autism spectrum can find meaningful employment, navigate real barriers, and build a future where they are not just supported but truly contributing.

From Preparation to Participation

The Journey So Far

For years, the path has been about preparation. Learning to communicate. Building routines. Developing independence. Each step carefully leading forward one milestone at a time.

The Question Now Changes

Eventually, the world opens up. And the question shifts from *how do we prepare?* to *how will my child participate?* This is not just a milestone it is the beginning of a new chapter in the lifelong journey toward independence and belonging.

Work is where preparation meets possibility. The goal has always been pointing here.

The Meaning of Work

Work is often seen as a necessity a way to earn, a way to sustain life. But it is so much more than that. For individuals on the autism spectrum, employment fulfills a deeper human need.

Structure

Predictable routines and clear expectations that align with how many autistic individuals naturally thrive.

Identity

A role and title that says: *I contribute. I belong here.* Work becomes part of who you are.

Contribution

The satisfaction of producing something of value felt by every person, regardless of ability.

Connection

A bridge to society a way of participating in the world alongside others.

> Work answers a deeper need: **to belong.**

Strengths That Deserve Recognition

Many individuals on the autism spectrum bring remarkable strengths to the workplace strengths that are often overlooked in traditional hiring contexts. In the right environment, these are not just helpful. They are genuinely valuable.

Deep Focus

The ability to concentrate intensely on a task, sustaining attention far beyond what most can manage.

Attention to Detail

Noticing what others miss catching errors, maintaining precision, ensuring quality.

Consistency

Showing up with dependability. Once a routine is established, it is upheld with remarkable steadiness.

Logical Thinking

Approaching problems with clear, systematic reasoning often seeing solutions others overlook.

Pattern Recognition

Identifying trends, sequences, and structures with exceptional accuracy and speed.

The Gap Between Ability and Opportunity

Despite these real and documented strengths, access to employment remains a significant challenge for many autistic individuals. The barrier is rarely a lack of ability it is a mismatch between how hiring works and how autistic individuals work best.

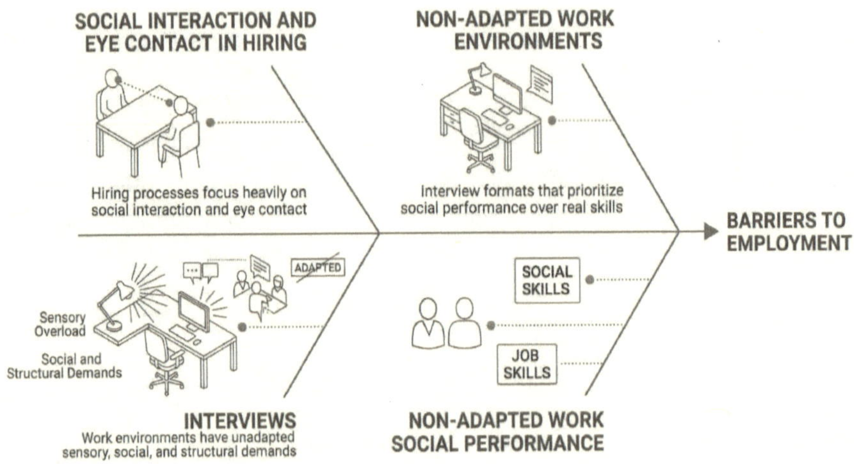

⚠ As a result of these systemic barriers, many capable individuals remain excluded not because they cannot do the work, but because the system was not designed with them in mind.

Rethinking What a Career Can Be

Traditional definitions of career a fixed path, a linear progression can feel limiting. For individuals on the autism spectrum, the path may look different. And that difference is not a limitation. It is a redefinition.

Structured Employment

A traditional job with clear responsibilities, consistent hours, and defined expectations often the best fit when the right support is in place.

Skill-Based Roles

Positions built around a specific talent or technical ability data entry, lab work, coding, design where depth of skill matters more than social breadth.

Flexible & Independent Paths

Freelancing, remote work, or family-supported business arrangements that allow autonomy and reduce social and sensory demands.

Entrepreneurship

Building something of one's own channeling deep interest and expertise into a focused venture, with support from family or mentors.

The form may vary. But the purpose remains: **meaningful engagement.**

Creating Supportive Work Environments

Employment success is not only about the individual it is equally about the environment. Small, intentional adaptations can make the difference between exclusion and flourishing. These are not major changes. But they create real accessibility.

Clear Instructions

Written, step-by-step guidance removes ambiguity and reduces anxiety around expectations.

Predictable Routines

Consistent schedules and advance notice of changes allow for confident, comfortable performance.

Reduced Sensory Load

Quieter workspaces, adjustable lighting, or noise-cancelling options remove distracting stimuli.

Supportive Supervision

Patient, direct feedback from a designated mentor builds trust and guides growth over time.

The Role of Employers

Organizations are beginning to recognize the value of neurodiversity. Some have introduced inclusive hiring programs, role-specific training, and structured onboarding.

But this is still evolving. Awareness is growing but not yet widespread. Every employer who takes one step forward changes what is possible for one more individual.

- Neurodiversity hiring programs are proven to improve team performance, retention, and innovation.

A Future That Is Possible

The path may be different. It may take more time, more effort, more adaptation. In India, employment opportunities for autistic individuals are still limited challenged by lack of structured programs, limited employer awareness, and social stigma. But change is beginning. Startups, NGOs, and forward-thinking organizations are building inclusive models.

Redefine Success

Success is not only position, salary, or status. It is engagement, comfort, and meaningful contribution. A role that fits the individual is more valuable than one that fits expectations.

Family as Foundation

Families identify opportunities, provide initial support, and help navigate challenges. Over time, the goal shifts: from support toward independence.

The Emotional Value

When an individual contributes, they feel seen. Work builds confidence, self-worth, and social identity not just productivity.

> **Work is not just about earning a living. It is about having a place in the world.**
> And every individual with the right support deserves that place.

Chapter 25

Supported Living Models

Creating a Life Beyond Dependence a compassionate, practical guide for parents and caregivers navigating one of the most profound questions of the autism journey: *What happens when I am not there?*

The Question No Parent Wants to Ask But Must

For years, the journey has been about support. Being there. Guiding. Protecting. Every step taken together.

But time moves forward. And with it comes a difficult, necessary thought: *How will my child live independently or with support over the long term?*

This is not just about housing. It is about life. It is about dignity, belonging, and the quiet courage it takes to plan for a future you may not always be present for.

> This question, though hard to ask, is one of the most loving things a parent can explore because asking it is the first step toward answering it.

Independence Does Not Mean Isolation

The idea of independent living is often misunderstood. It does not mean living alone without help, or managing everything without support.

What it *does* mean	What it does *not* mean
• Living with dignity and choice • Making decisions about one's own life • Being part of a community	• Going without support entirely • Managing every task alone • Being disconnected from family or care

For some individuals, this may look like full independence. For others, it may involve structured, ongoing support. And both are equally valid paths forward.

Different Models of Supported Living

Supported living exists in many forms each designed to meet different levels of need. There is no single "best" model. Only what fits the individual.

Independent Living

Living alone or with minimal support, managing daily life independently with occasional check-ins.

Supported Living

Living in a shared or assisted environment, receiving help with specific tasks while retaining autonomy.

Family-Based Living

Continuing to live with family while building increasing levels of independence within the home.

Assisted Care Settings

Structured environments with professional support for individuals requiring higher levels of assistance.

Daily Life & The Emotional Journey of Transition

What a Supported Environment Provides

- Structured daily routines
- Opportunities for independence
- Access to support when needed
- Personal care and household skills
- Social interaction and community

The goal is not dependency. It is **supported autonomy** a life shaped by the individual, held steady by a caring structure.

For Parents: A Range of Emotions

Letting go even partially is not easy. There will be moments of doubt and fear. But there can also be profound pride, relief, and hope.

You may feel

Concern · Doubt · Fear of the unknown

You may also feel

Pride · Relief · Hope · Gratitude

Because independence, even with support, is always a step forward.

Safety, Community & the Individual's Perspective

Safety & Structure

Supported living models must ensure physical safety, emotional well-being, and clear routines. Structure provides stability and stability builds confidence over time.

Sense of Belonging

Living is not only about space it is about connection. Neighbors, peers, and support networks create the sense of belonging that is essential to a meaningful life.

The Individual's Voice

For the individual, supported living offers a sense of identity, personal space, and opportunity to grow a shift from being cared for to participating in one's own life.

The Reality in India & Planning for the Future

Where Things Stand

In India, supported living models are still developing. Many families continue to provide lifelong care which reflects enormous strength, but also highlights the urgent need for more options.

Key Challenges

- Limited structured programs
- Cultural preference for family care
- Low awareness of alternatives

How to Begin Planning

Long-term planning is essential even if it feels distant. Planning does not mean rushing. It means preparing with intention and care.

1 Explore available options

Research local and national programs, residential models, and government schemes.

2 Build life skills early

Daily independence starts with small, consistent practice at home.

3 Create support networks

Identify people beyond family who can be part of your child's future circle of support.

Redefining What It Means to Live Well

> A life well-lived is not defined by how independently it is lived but by how meaningfully it is experienced.

Living well is not about independence alone. It is about comfort, stability, meaningful engagement, and respect. Each individual defines it differently and every definition deserves to be honored.

Comfort

A space that feels safe and familiar

Stability

Routines and structures that anchor daily life

Engagement

Meaningful activities and relationships

Respect

Choices honored, dignity preserved

Chapter 26

Autism Ecosystem: A Systems View

There is a point in every journey when individual effort begins to meet systemic reality. A parent has learned, adapted, and supported their child step by step. And yet, something still feels difficult not because of lack of effort, but because the system itself is not aligned. This chapter examines the autism ecosystem as a whole: its gaps, its potential, and the path from fragmentation to design.

When Effort Meets Fragmentation

Families navigating autism support don't move through a single, unified system. They move through many often disconnected from one another. Healthcare, therapy, education, and social structures each exist and each functions. But rarely together.

Healthcare

Diagnosis, medical management, and specialist referrals often the entry point, rarely the connector.

Therapy

Speech, occupational, behavioral each delivered by different providers with different goals.

Education

IEPs, classroom supports, and specialized programs that vary widely by school and region.

Social Structures

Community, peer support, and family networks that provide context but rarely receive coordination.

⚠ In a fragmented system, **parents become the connection point** carrying information, bridging gaps, and trying to create continuity that the system itself does not provide.

The Illusion of Availability

At first glance, support seems to exist. There are therapists, schools, policies, and programs. But availability is not the same as accessibility and accessibility is not the same as integration. A system can exist and still not work.

Availability

Services and supports that exist in theory listed, funded, or legislated.

Accessibility → Integration

The critical leap most systems fail to make. A service that exists but cannot be reached or that doesn't connect to other services provides only partial value. True support requires all three levels working in concert.

- Can the family find it?
- Can they afford it?
- Does it connect to everything else?

What Is an Ecosystem And What Is It Today?

An ecosystem is not just a collection of parts. It is a network of connections where each element communicates, aligns, and supports the other. In nature, ecosystems thrive on balance. In support systems, they thrive on coordination.

An Ideal Ecosystem

Connected

Information flows seamlessly across providers

Coordinated

Goals are shared and progress is tracked together

Continuous

Support adapts across life stages without gaps

Today's Reality

Fragmented

Services operate in silos without shared communication

Reactive

Support responds to crises rather than anticipating needs

Uneven

Quality and access vary dramatically by geography

Families move from diagnosis to therapy to school to support groups each transition requiring new understanding, new effort, and new adaptation. This is not a seamless journey. It is a series of disconnected steps.

The Missing Link: Integration & The Burden on Families

The most critical gap in the autism ecosystem is not the absence of services it is the **absence of connection between them**. Without integration, progress slows not because the child cannot grow, but because the system does not support continuity.

No Shared Goals

Therapists, educators, and healthcare providers rarely align on unified outcomes for the child, leading to inconsistent approaches.

Isolated Data

Assessments and evaluations exist but are rarely shared or used to guide long-term decisions across providers.

Burden Shifts to Families

When systems fail to connect, parents absorb the coordination role becoming full-time advocates, decision-makers, and case managers.

> The system should carry the structure not the individual. Sustained family coordination is a symptom of systemic failure, not a feature of good support.

Urban vs. Rural Policy vs. Practice

The autism ecosystem is not only fragmented by service type it is fragmented by geography. Access to support is profoundly shaped by where a family lives, creating a disparity not in need, but in opportunity.

Urban Areas

- Greater concentration of specialists
- Higher public awareness
- More program availability
- Competitive waitlists

Rural Areas

- Limited therapist availability
- Lower community awareness
- Fewer trained professionals
- Long travel distances to services

Policies are often in place. Frameworks are defined. Rights are established. But implementation varies between regions, between institutions creating inconsistency. And inconsistency creates uncertainty for every family trying to plan ahead.

The Need for a Lifecycle Approach

Autism is not a phase. It is a lifelong journey. Which means support must extend across every stage of life yet most systems concentrate heavily on early intervention and leave significant gaps in later years.

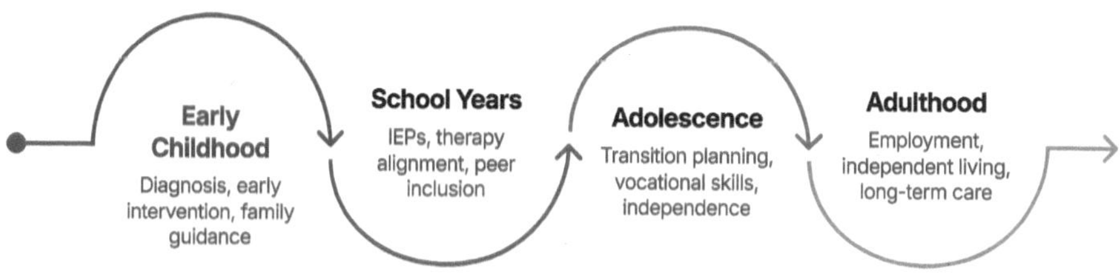

The systems that support early childhood are far more developed than those that support adults. Employment pathways, independent living programs, and long-term care frameworks remain underdeveloped leaving families navigating adulthood with little systemic guidance and significant uncertainty.

> ⓘ A lifecycle approach means designing support that **anticipates transitions** not just responds to them. Each stage must connect meaningfully to the next.

From Fragmentation to Design Building What's Next

The next step is not to add more components to the ecosystem. It is to design the system — to move from availability to integration, from support to structure, from individual effort to collective efficiency. Technology, coordinated care, and purposeful policy all play a role.

Shared Platforms

Technology that connects diagnosis, therapy, and education data across providers — enabling coordinated decision-making.

Integrated Care Plans

Unified goals set collaboratively by all professionals supporting a child — tracked and adapted over time.

Lifecycle Continuity

Systems that follow the individual across stages — from early childhood through adulthood — without requiring families to rebuild from scratch.

Policy Into Practice

Closing the gap between legislated rights and lived reality — through accountability, training, and equitable distribution of resources.

> *"A child's progress should not depend on how well a family navigates the system. It should depend on how well the system supports the child."*
>
> When that shift happens, the journey becomes not just possible — but sustainable.

Chapter 27

Government Policies & Rights

What exists, what reaches, and what truly matters: a compassionate guide to understanding how policy shapes everyday life for autistic individuals and their families in India and beyond.

What Policy Means in Real Life

Policies are often seen as distant documents, frameworks, and announcements. But in reality, they shape everyday experience in deeply personal ways. For families navigating autism support, policy is not abstract. It is profoundly practical.

Who Gets Access

Policies determine eligibility which families qualify for support and under what conditions.

What Support Exists

From education to healthcare, policy defines the landscape of available resources.

How Systems Respond

The speed, clarity, and consistency of institutional response is shaped by policy design.

> There is a moment in every parent's journey when the focus shifts from understanding the child... to understanding the system.

The Promise of Rights

Across the world, there has been growing recognition of neurodiversity. With that recognition comes the foundational idea of rights not optional privileges, but fundamental entitlements that every individual deserves.

Education

Every child's right to learn in an environment designed to meet their needs.

Healthcare

Access to appropriate medical, therapeutic, and developmental support.

Equal Opportunity

The right to participate fully in education, employment, and community life.

Dignified Living

A life of respect, safety, and meaningful participation in society.

The Policy Landscape in India

India has established significant policy frameworks to support individuals with autism. The landmark **Rights of Persons with Disabilities Act, 2016 (RPWD Act)** formally recognizes autism as a disability and creates a legal foundation for support across multiple life domains.

The Act provides provisions spanning education, employment, social inclusion, and legal rights. Certification systems also enable families to access government benefits and services though navigating them can be complex.

> ⓘ The RPWD Act, 2016 was a turning point it moved autism from the margins of policy into a recognized, rights-based framework.

Key Provisions Under RPWD Act

- Recognition of autism as a specified disability
- Right to free and inclusive education
- Employment reservation in government sectors
- Social security and financial assistance
- Legal guardianship provisions
- Disability certification enabling service access

When Rights Exist But Access Is Uneven

In many systems, policies are well defined. But lived experience varies between regions, institutions, and implementation practices. A right on paper does not always translate to a right in practice. Families often find themselves navigating this gap.

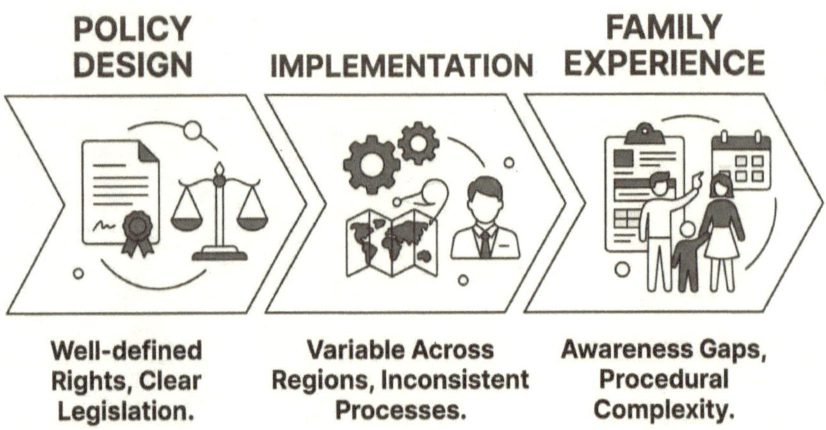

⚠ The most consistent challenge is not policy creation it is policy execution. A system may exist, but if processes are unclear and awareness is low, the benefit does not reach those who need it.

Education, Certification & Financial Support

Three pillars of practical policy education inclusion, disability certification, and financial benefits form the backbone of government support for autistic individuals and their families.

Inclusive Education

Schools are expected to admit children with disabilities, provide necessary support, and create accessible learning environments. Implementation varies some schools adapt well, while others require family advocacy.

Disability Certification

Access to most government benefits requires a disability certificate, obtained through medical assessment and documentation. For some families it is straightforward; for others, delays and procedural challenges create barriers.

Financial Benefits

Provisions exist for financial assistance, subsidies, and scholarships but awareness is often limited. Many families remain unaware of what they are entitled to or how to access it, reducing the real-world impact of these policies.

The Role of Awareness & Advocacy

Policies are only effective when people know about them. And real progress often happens not because policies change first but because communities and families push for change from the ground up.

Awareness Must Exist at Every Level

- **Families** understanding entitlements and how to access them
- **Schools & Employers** knowing their obligations under the law
- **Local Authorities** implementing and communicating programs consistently

Advocacy Drives Real Change

Parents, organizations, and communities raise awareness, push for implementation, and create accountability. Change is often gradual but it is driven by persistence.

Every family that learns their rights and advocates for them contributes to a stronger, more responsive system for everyone.

From Rights to Reality

The goal is not to create more policies. It is to make existing ones work to move from design to delivery, from access to usability, from rights on paper to rights in daily life. When systems truly deliver on those rights, families move from struggle to support.

Design

Legislation and frameworks that recognize and protect rights

Delivery

Clear processes, trained staff, and consistent implementation

Access

Families aware of, and able to navigate, the support available

Reality

Rights experienced in daily life reducing burden and enabling belonging

> Rights are meaningful only when they are experienced. Not in documents but in daily life.

Chapter 28

Economics of Autism Care

The Cost Behind the Journey

There are conversations families rarely have openly. Not because they are unimportant but because they are difficult. One of them is about cost. Beneath every therapy session, every specialist visit, and every specialized tool lies a financial reality that shapes decisions every single day. This chapter explores that reality with honesty, clarity, and compassion.

The Invisible Layer of the Journey

From the outside, autism is often understood through behavior, therapy, and education. But beneath all of this lies another layer: **the financial reality**.

It does not appear in diagnosis reports. It is not always discussed in therapy sessions. And yet, it shapes decisions every single day. Families navigating autism care must simultaneously manage emotional complexity and financial pressure, often without a clear roadmap.

> The financial reality of autism care is invisible in clinical conversations, yet it is one of the most powerful forces shaping a family's journey.

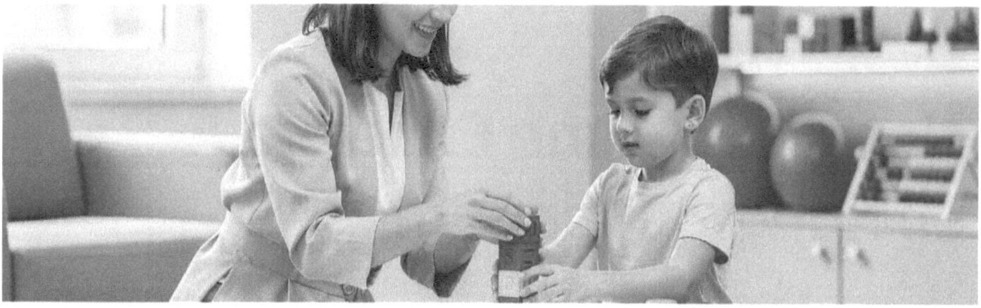

When Support Comes with a Price

After diagnosis, families begin to explore support systems. Each intervention is essential. Each is impactful. But each also comes with a cost and over time, these costs accumulate significantly.

Speech Therapy

Regular sessions to build communication skills and language development over months and years.

Occupational Therapy

Developing fine motor skills, sensory processing, and daily life independence.

Behavioral Interventions

Structured programs like ABA that require consistent, intensive professional engagement.

Specialized Education

Tailored schooling environments or shadow teachers, often privately arranged and funded.

Not a One-Time Expense A Lifelong Continuum

Unlike many medical conditions, autism care is not short-term. Support may be needed at every stage of life, transforming cost into a long-term commitment not a phase, but a journey.

1. Early Childhood

Diagnosis, early intervention therapies, and developmental support.

2. School Years

Specialized education, shadow teachers, IEPs, and ongoing therapies.

3. Adolescence

Social skills development, vocational training, and transition planning.

4. Adulthood

Supported living, employment assistance, and continued care needs.

> ⓘ This lifelong continuum means families must think not in terms of months, but decades making financial planning a critical part of the autism care journey.

The Full Scope of Financial Impact

Financial impact extends well beyond therapy fees. Families often carry a wide range of costs that are rarely acknowledged in formal discussions about autism care.

Direct Costs

- Speech, occupational, and behavioral therapy fees
- Specialized school tuition or shadow teacher fees
- Diagnostic assessments and specialist consultations
- Assistive tools, apps, and learning materials

Hidden & Indirect Costs

- Travel to clinics and therapy centers
- Time taken off work for appointments
- Career reduction or full stop by a caregiver
- Home modifications for sensory needs

⚠ In many cases, one parent reduces working hours or stops working altogether. Not out of preference, but out of necessity.

The Emotional Weight of Financial Decisions

Money, in this context, is not just a number. It carries emotion. Families face a uniquely painful intersection where financial constraints meet deeply personal decisions about their child's wellbeing.

Guilt

Am I doing enough? Should I be spending more?

Pressure

Every trade-off feels like it could impact a child's progress.

Uncertainty

No clear timeline or defined endpoint creates ongoing financial anxiety.

These questions are not just financial. They are deeply personal and they deserve acknowledgment, not silence.

The Reality in India

In India, much of autism care is privately funded. This creates a landscape of uneven access where need is equal, but opportunity is not.

Urban India

Available Services: Many Specialized Centers

Cost: Higher Fees, More Options

Insurance: Limited Coverage, More Awareness

Support Networks: NGOs, Parent Groups

Rural India

Available Services: Very Few Options

Cost: Lower Fees, Scarce Services

Insurance: Minimal to None

Support Networks: Informal Family Networks

> This disparity does not exist in need every family needs support equally. It exists in access. Closing that gap is one of the most urgent priorities in autism policy in India.

Policy, Community & Rethinking Value

Building a more equitable autism care landscape requires action on multiple fronts from government policy to grassroots community support, and a fundamental reframing of how we define value in care.

Government & Policy

Financial assistance schemes and subsidies exist but awareness and accessibility remain the critical gap. Families often cannot navigate the process.

NGOs & Support Networks

Community-based organizations offer affordable services, shared guidance, and emotional solidarity reducing both financial and personal burden.

High-Value, Low-Cost Support

Structured routines, parent-led interaction, and consistent reinforcement at home require time not necessarily financial investment yet carry enormous impact.

Early Investment as Value

Early support improves communication, builds independence, and reduces long-term dependency transforming cost into meaningful, measurable value.

> The journey of autism care carries a cost. But it also carries value far beyond numbers. When systems evolve to support that journey, the burden becomes lighter, and the path becomes clearer.

Chapter 29
Building Scalable Models
From Individual Effort to Systemic Impact

Across cities, towns, and communities, the same story repeats: families struggle, learn, adapt, and find a path only for the next family to begin from zero. This chapter examines what it truly means to build autism support systems that scale reaching not just some, but all.

The Repetition of Struggle

> A family struggles. Learns. Adapts. Finds a path through effort, persistence, and resilience. And then another family begins the same journey. From the beginning.

Parents search for answers. They navigate fragmented systems, learn through trial and error, and build their own solutions. Each family's hard-won knowledge rarely transfers to the next. The effort is repeated, not inherited. The system does not change only the people bearing the burden of it.

Individual Discovery

Each family reinvents the wheel finding therapists, schools, and strategies on their own.

Fragmented Systems

Support exists in pockets, but is rarely connected, consistent, or accessible to all.

No Institutional Memory

When solutions are not codified, hard-won insights disappear rather than compound over time.

When Solutions Do Not Scale

There are many good efforts in the autism support landscape. Dedicated therapists. Supportive schools. Strong NGOs. Each creates real, meaningful impact but often only for those within reach. The model works for some, but not for all. And that limitation is structural, not motivational.

The Dedicated Therapist

Deep expertise, but limited reach. One professional can support only so many families at once.

The Supportive School

A beacon in one community but its model rarely spreads beyond its own walls.

The Strong NGO

Ground-level trust and connection but funding cycles and geography constrain expansion.

What Does "Scalable" Really Mean?

Scalability is not simply about growth in numbers. It is the ability to reach more people, maintain quality across diverse contexts, and reduce dependency on individual heroics. A truly scalable model works not just in one place but across many. Not just for one family but for thousands.

Reach

Extending support to families who have never had access before urban and rural alike.

Quality

Maintaining standards of support even as the model expands beyond its original champions.

Reduced Dependency

Building systems that function reliably without requiring exceptional individuals at every node.

The Architecture of Scale

Scaling autism support is uniquely complex because needs are diverse, individualized, and context-dependent. What works for one child may not work for another. Standardization alone cannot be the answer. What is needed instead are **adaptable frameworks** structures that define what support looks like, how it is delivered, and how it evolves while remaining flexible enough to serve each family's reality.

STRUCTURED FRAMEWORKS

- Define support looks like
- How delivered
- How it evolves

PUBLIC-PRIVATE COLLABORATION

- Governments: policy & reach
- Private: innovation
- NGOs: community trust

MEASUREMENT FOR OUTCOMES

- Improved communication
- Increased independence
- Quality of life (not just numbers)

Bridging the Urban-Rural Divide

Urban Areas

Services exist but access is often limited by cost, waitlists, and awareness. Proximity does not guarantee equity.

- High cost of specialized therapy
- Long waitlists at quality providers
- Uneven distribution across neighborhoods

Rural Areas

Need is present and growing but services are sparse, professionals are few, and distances are vast.

- Limited local expertise and specialists
- No nearby diagnostic or intervention centers
- Families bear the cost of travel and time

Scalable models must address both realities. The path forward involves extending reach through technology, reducing cost through community training, and adapting delivery to match where families actually live.

Technology and Training as Multipliers

Two forces, when combined, can exponentially expand the reach of autism support: technology and training. Technology connects families to resources, enables remote intervention, and standardizes foundational tools. Training multiplies human capacity empowering parents, teachers, and community workers to deliver consistent, informed support. Neither alone is sufficient. Together, they are transformative.

Remote Support Technology

Teletherapy, digital assessment tools, and app-based programs bring intervention to families regardless of location.

Parent & Caregiver Training

When parents are equipped with structured knowledge, they become daily agents of support reducing reliance on scarce professionals.

Educator Capacity Building

Teachers and school staff trained in autism-informed practices extend support into eight hours of a child's daily environment.

Community Worker Networks

Front-line community workers, when trained and supported, become the last-mile connectors that no system can otherwise reach.

The Reality in India and the Path Forward

India presents both the urgency and the opportunity most clearly. A vast population, deeply uneven access to services, and growing public awareness create the conditions for transformative scale if models are designed thoughtfully. The challenge is not a lack of need. It is designing systems that are affordable, culturally adaptive, and sustainable without depending on extraordinary individual effort.

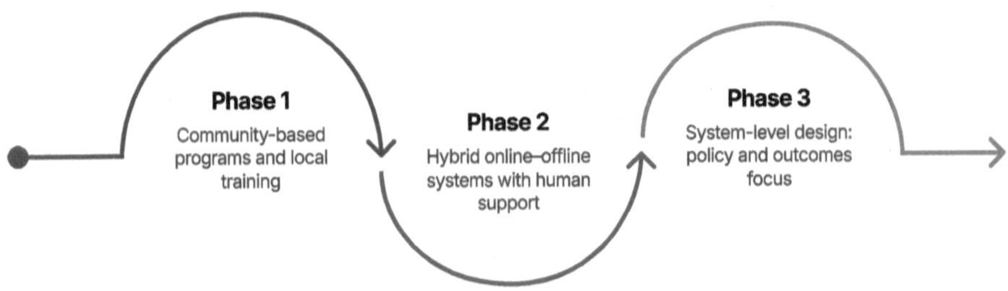

The goal is clear: No family should have to start from zero. Every family deserves access to guidance, structured support, and clear pathways from the very beginning.

True impact is not measured by how well we solve a problem once but by how many people we enable to solve it, consistently. When systems are designed to scale, support becomes not limited but widespread.

Chapter 30

Role of AI in Autism Support

There was a time when support depended entirely on people a parent's observation, a therapist's experience, a teacher's intuition. Each is valuable. Each is essential. But also limited by time, access, and human capacity. This chapter explores how artificial intelligence is entering deeply human spaces and what that means for the children and families we support.

Seeing Patterns Humans May Miss

One of AI's greatest strengths is its capacity for pattern recognition across time, across data, across subtle signals that may not yet be visible to the human eye. For children on the autism spectrum, this carries meaningful implications.

Behavioral Analysis Over Time

AI systems can continuously analyze behavioral data, identifying trends and shifts that emerge gradually often too slowly for daily observation to catch.

Subtle Communication Shifts

Small changes in response patterns, vocabulary use, or social engagement can signal important developmental moments surfaced earlier with AI support.

Early Developmental Indicators

Patterns that might take months to notice clinically can be flagged by AI tools in shorter windows, enabling earlier conversations and interventions.

Early Identification A New Possibility

Early identification is one of the most powerful determinants of long-term outcomes in autism support. Yet it often depends on a convergence of awareness, specialist access, and timely evaluation resources that are not equally distributed.

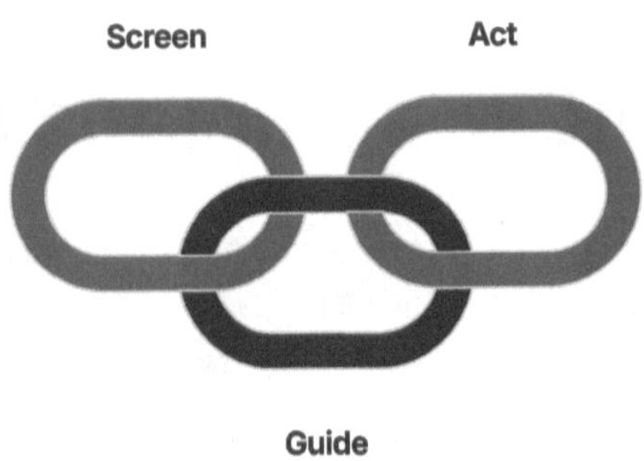

AI holds the potential to extend the reach of early identification not by replacing trained professionals, but by equipping them with earlier, more consistent signals. The result is a system where no child waits simply because the right person wasn't available at the right time.

Personalized Learning at Scale

Every child learns differently yet traditional educational systems are often built for uniformity. AI introduces something the classroom has rarely been able to offer: genuine adaptability, delivered consistently, at scale.

What Traditional Systems Offer

- Uniform pace for all learners
- Fixed curriculum structure
- Teacher-dependent differentiation
- Periodic progress assessment

What AI-Enabled Learning Adds

- Pace adjusted in real time
- Content modified to individual patterns
- Consistent, data-informed adaptation
- Continuous progress monitoring

This creates something powerful: personalization that does not depend solely on one teacher, one session, or one lucky moment of connection. It scales what good teaching aspires to be.

Supporting Communication & Behavioral Insight

AI-Enabled Communication Tools

For children who struggle to express themselves, AI-powered tools can predict communicative intent, suggest words or phrases, and enhance AAC systems making expression more accessible and reducing frustration.

Objective Behavioral Observation

AI observes without bias or assumption. It can track triggers, analyze behavioral patterns across contexts, and suggest targeted interventions providing data-rich insights that support human understanding rather than replace it.

Strengthening Connection

When communication barriers decrease, connection deepens. AI tools act as a bridge freeing children to express more, and freeing caregivers to respond with greater understanding and confidence.

The Risks, Ethics, and Responsibilities

With every powerful tool comes a responsibility to use it wisely. As AI enters sensitive spaces like autism support, we must hold two truths at once: its potential is significant, and its risks are real.

⚠️ Risk of Over-Reliance

Autism support is not only about accuracy it is about connection, empathy, and trust. These cannot be automated. The danger is replacing human presence with digital response.

🔒 Data Privacy

How is sensitive behavioral data stored, shared, and used? Who has access? AI systems must be designed with explicit protections for the dignity and privacy of every child and family.

⚖️ Equity of Access

AI tools risk deepening existing inequalities if only accessible to affluent families. Ethical implementation demands that affordability and access be built into design not treated as afterthoughts.

⚠️ AI must be designed not just for efficiency but for dignity. The standard is not what technology can do. It is what it should do.

The Reality in India & The Road Ahead

In India, AI adoption in autism support is still emerging. Growing interest, early-stage innovation, and increasing mobile platform accessibility represent genuine momentum alongside real challenges that must be addressed thoughtfully.

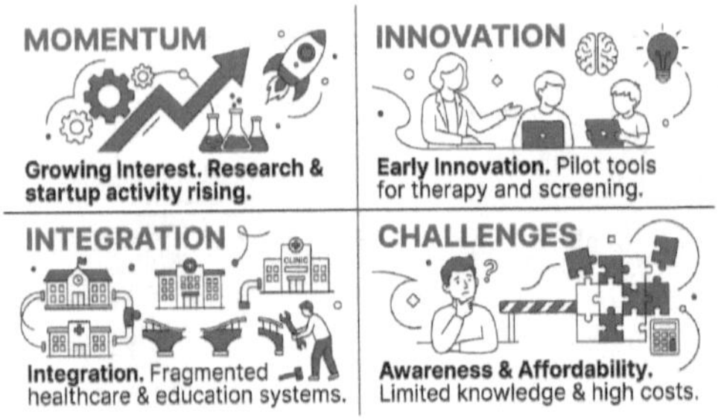

From Tool to Ecosystem

AI's greatest potential is not as a standalone product but as connective tissue within a larger support system. Linking diagnosis, therapy, education, and progress tracking into a continuous, coherent experience reduces fragmentation and increases impact for every family it serves.

> ⓘ The opportunity in India is significant. But it requires thoughtful, equitable, and culturally-sensitive implementation to fulfill its promise.

A Future That Assists, Not Replaces

> Technology does not replace understanding. But it can deepen it. And when used with care, it becomes not just intelligent but meaningful.

The goal of AI in autism support is not to take over. It is to reduce burden, increase clarity, and enable better decisions so that the humans at the center of care can show up more fully, more informed, and more empowered.

Human remains at the center

A parent's understanding, a teacher's empathy, a therapist's judgment these anchor every system AI supports.

AI extends human capacity

Pattern recognition, personalization, and early identification augment what professionals and caregivers can do not what they are.

Ethics guides implementation

Privacy, dignity, equity, and access must be foundational not add-ons in every AI system built for children and families.

The next frontier: Digital Therapeutics & Wearables

Technology's role in daily life continues to evolve. The next chapter explores how digital therapeutics and wearable devices extend support into every moment of a child's day.

Chapter 31

Digital Therapeutics & Wearables

When Support Becomes Continuous

There are moments parents come to recognize over time, not dramatic ones and not always visible to others, but deeply significant. A child who becomes overwhelmed suddenly. A shift in mood without warning. A behavior that seems to come from nowhere. And the question that follows, almost instinctively: *If only I could understand what is happening before it happens.*

The Limits of Observation

For years, understanding has depended on observation. Watching closely. Learning patterns. Anticipating triggers. Parents become experts in noticing attuned to the smallest shifts in expression, posture, and energy.

But even the most attentive observation has limits. Because not everything can be seen. Some changes begin quietly, long before behavior appears on the surface.

Rising Stress

Internal tension builds gradually invisible to even the closest observer.

Sensory Overload

Subtle overstimulation accumulates before it becomes visible behavior.

Emotional Build-Up

By the time a reaction appears, the internal experience has already escalated.

Wearables: Listening to What We Cannot See

Wearable devices add a profound new layer to caregiving. They do not rely on visible behavior. Instead, they track physiological signals that often change *before* behavior does offering an early window into a child's internal experience.

Heart Rate Monitoring

A rising heart rate may indicate growing stress a signal that arrives before any outward sign appears.

Movement Patterns

Changes in movement and activity levels can signal discomfort or sensory overload in the making.

Physiological Signals

Subtle body cues temperature, galvanic skin response serve as early indicators of what may come next.

These are not conclusions they are indicators. Early signs that open the door to timely, gentle support.

From Reaction to Anticipation

The Old Model

Traditionally, support has been reactive. A behavior appears. A response follows. Caregivers and therapists act after the moment has already arrived often when regulation is already difficult.

The New Possibility

With digital tools, anticipation becomes possible. Recognizing patterns early. Intervening before escalation. Not to control behavior but to support regulation at the right moment.

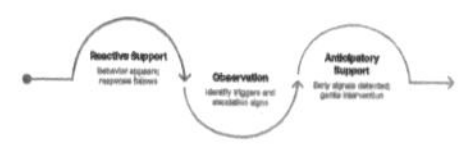

This shift from reaction to anticipation is one of the most meaningful changes digital therapeutics bring to everyday caregiving.

What Are Digital Therapeutics?

Digital therapeutics represent a genuinely new approach not apps built for convenience, but tools designed specifically for therapeutic intervention. They aim to support behavior, reinforce learning, and guide responses in real time. Unlike traditional methods, they do not wait for a scheduled session.

Behavior Support

Structured digital prompts help children navigate challenging moments with consistent, familiar guidance.

Real-Time Guidance

In-the-moment tools breathing exercises, calming visuals activate exactly when needed, not after the fact.

Reinforced Learning

Therapeutic concepts are woven into everyday digital interactions, creating continuous reinforcement beyond therapy sessions.

A Quiet Intervention For Child and Caregiver

What makes these tools uniquely valuable is their subtlety. They do not interrupt loudly. They do not demand attention. They work in the background, offering small nudges at precisely the right moment.

For the Child

- → A gentle haptic alert before overwhelm peaks
- → A quiet suggestion to take a calming break
- → A soft signal that a shift in environment may help

For the Caregiver

- → Insight into patterns that are hard to observe directly
- → Awareness of what is happening before a crisis point
- → Guidance on what to do in uncertain moments

> One of the hardest parts of caregiving is not knowing: *Why is this happening? What should I do now?* These tools reduce that uncertainty quietly, consistently.

Important Considerations

With every advancement comes responsibility. As these tools become more capable, it is essential to hold space for the questions they raise about measurement, privacy, and the irreplaceable human dimension of caregiving.

⚖️ The Risk of Over-Measurement

Not every moment needs to be tracked. Some moments need to be *experienced*. When every signal becomes data, there is a risk of over-monitoring and losing the natural flow of human interaction.

🔒 Privacy & Dignity

These tools collect behavioral patterns, physiological data, and daily activity insights. Who owns this data? How is it used and protected? Support must never come at the cost of a child's dignity.

❤️ The Human Dimension

A child is not a system to be optimized they are an individual to be understood. Technology can support, but it must never replace human connection, emotional presence, or intuitive understanding.

The Reality in India & The Road Ahead

Where We Are Today

In India, adoption of digital therapeutics and wearables is still emerging. Access is growing but remains uneven. Challenges of cost, awareness, and integration with existing care systems mean that these tools are not yet equally available to all families.

Yet the potential is significant. Especially in areas where access to specialists is limited, these technologies can serve as a vital bridge connecting families to support that would otherwise be out of reach.

A Companion, Not a Replacement

These technologies are not the solution. They are a support system a companion in the journey. They connect moments: between therapy sessions, between school and home, between observation and action. They create continuity where there was only disconnection.

Support does not always need to be visible to be effective. Sometimes the most powerful support is the one that is present quietly, consistently, continuously.

Chapter 32

Building an Integrated Autism Platform

There is a moment, somewhere along the journey, when a quiet realization settles in not about the child, not about the effort, but about the system itself. Everything exists. And yet, everything feels disconnected. This chapter explores what it means to move from fragments to flow: building an integrated platform that brings therapy, school, and home together into one living, evolving understanding of a child.

The Experience of Fragmentation

A parent moves through the day a therapy session in the morning, a school update in the afternoon, a behavior challenge at home in the evening. Each moment meaningful. Each piece important. But none of them fully connected.

Reports

Assessment documents and session notes held by different providers, rarely shared across settings.

Conversations

Verbal updates between therapists, teachers, and parents that are never formally captured.

Observations

Daily behavioral patterns noticed at home that never reach the clinical or school team.

Memory

Parents carry the entire history of their child's journey in their heads an unsustainable burden.

The core tension: The child is one but the system is many.

When Continuity Is Missing

Progress in autism support depends not just on what happens in one place, but on how everything comes together. A therapist may work on communication. A teacher may focus on learning. A parent may manage behavior. Without alignment, progress becomes uneven not because effort is lacking, but because connection is.

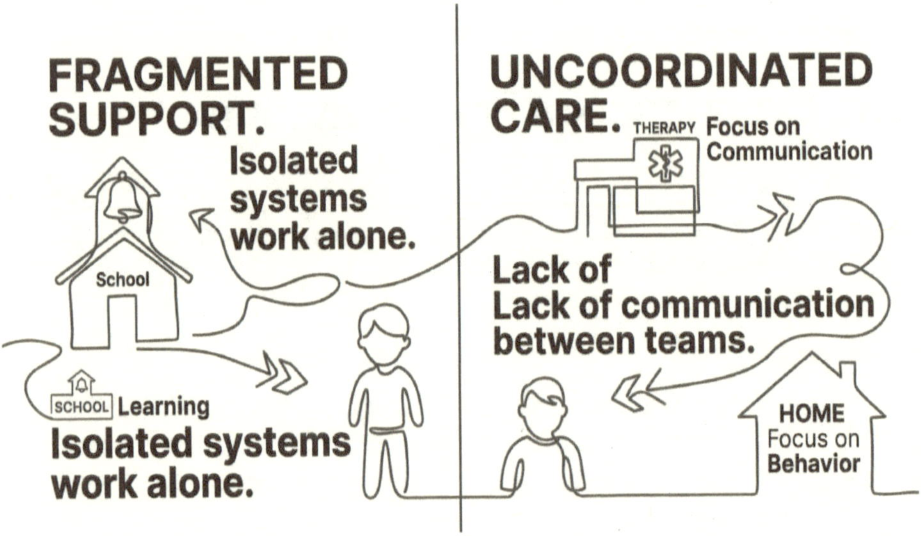

When these three worlds operate in isolation, the child must navigate the gaps and so must the family. Integration is not a luxury. It is a prerequisite for meaningful, consistent progress.

What Is an Integrated Platform?

An integrated platform is not just technology. It is a way of bringing everything together a shared space where information flows, insights connect, and decisions align. Where the journey is not fragmented, but continuous.

Information Flows

Data from every setting moves seamlessly to everyone who needs it no more siloed reports or lost updates.

Insights Connect

Patterns that would be invisible in isolation become clear when all data is viewed together in one place.

Decisions Align

Therapists, teachers, and parents work from the same understanding leading to more coordinated, effective support.

The Power of a Single View

Imagine a system where therapy progress is visible to teachers, classroom behavior informs therapy, and parent observations guide intervention not separately, but together. A single, evolving view of the child. Not static reports. But living understanding.

Today's Reality

- Separate portals for each provider
- Manual updates by parents
- Delayed access to progress data
- Decisions made in isolation

The Integrated Vision

- One shared view across all settings
- Automatic data synchronization
- Real-time progress visibility
- Coordinated, informed decisions

From Data to Meaning

Today, data exists everywhere assessment reports, session notes, school feedback. But data alone is not enough. What matters is meaning. An integrated system transforms raw information into actionable insight, helping every member of the support team understand what is truly happening for the child.

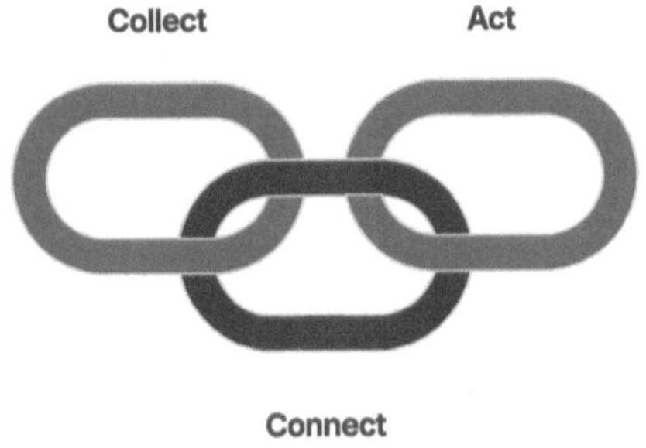

By identifying patterns across environments, highlighting what is working, and flagging what needs attention, an integrated platform turns the noise of fragmented information into a clear, coherent signal that drives better outcomes.

Reducing the Burden on Families

In the current system, parents hold everything together. They remember. They explain. They coordinate. Every appointment, every progress note, every behavioral shift lives in their memory because no system holds it for them.

1

Individual Effort

Parents manually track, recall, and relay critical information across every provider and setting.

2

System Design

The platform carries the coordination load, freeing parents to focus on what matters most their child.

When systems do the heavy lifting, families can show up with more presence, more energy, and more joy.

Real-Time Support, Not Delayed Response

One of the most powerful aspects of integration is timeliness. Instead of waiting for periodic reviews or delayed adjustments, support becomes continuous, responsive, and adaptive. Changes can be made when they matter most in the moment, not weeks later.

🔄 Continuous

Support does not pause between appointments. The system monitors and tracks around the clock.

📡 Responsive

When a pattern shifts, the right people are notified immediately no waiting for the next scheduled review.

🎯 Adaptive

Interventions can be adjusted in real time based on what the data reveals, not what was assumed months ago.

The Role of AI Within the Platform

Artificial Intelligence can enhance integration in meaningful ways detecting patterns across large datasets, suggesting personalized interventions, and predicting potential challenges before they escalate. But AI functions best as a guide, not a decision-maker. It supports human judgment rather than replacing it.

Pattern Detection

AI identifies behavioral and developmental patterns across environments that a human team might miss in fragmented data.

Personalized Suggestions

Based on a child's unique profile, AI can recommend intervention strategies tailored to their current needs and history.

Proactive Alerts

Rather than reacting to crises, AI can flag early warning signals enabling the team to intervene before challenges intensify.

Simplicity and Trust: The Non-Negotiables

For such a system to truly work, it must be simple enough for every stakeholder to use and trustworthy enough for every family to embrace. Complexity creates resistance. Simplicity enables adoption. And without trust, even the most powerful platform will be abandoned.

Simplicity

Designed for parents, teachers, and therapists not just tech-savvy users. Every feature must earn its place by being genuinely useful and easy to access.

- Intuitive interfaces for all users
- Minimal training required
- Accessible on any device

Trust & Privacy

When everything comes together, so does responsibility. An integrated platform must protect personal data, sensitive information, and family privacy at every level.

- End-to-end data encryption
- Granular permission controls
- Transparent data practices

Trust is not optional. It is the foundation upon which every other feature of the platform must be built.

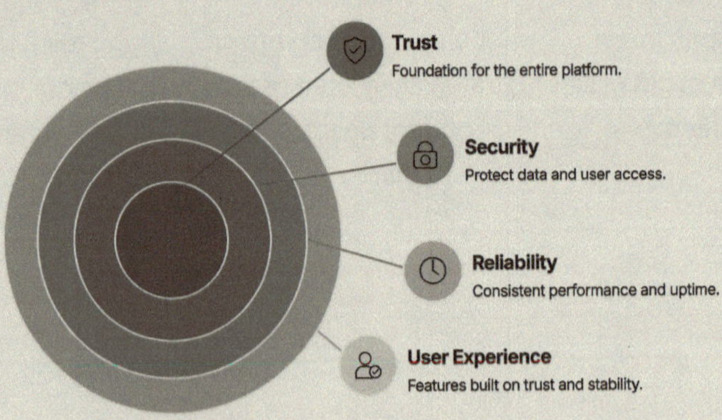

The Reality in India

In India, elements of integrated autism platforms are beginning to emerge but they remain fragmented, early-stage, and limited in scale. The gap between what is possible and what is available is significant. And yet, so is the opportunity.

1

Bridge the Gap

Connect urban centers of expertise with rural families who currently have little to no access to autism support services.

2

Reduce Physical Barriers

Move care beyond clinic walls through digital platforms that work on low-bandwidth connections and affordable devices.

3

Enable Continuity

Ensure that a child's support journey does not reset every time a provider changes or a family relocates.

From System to Experience A Shift in Thinking

Ultimately, the goal is not to build a platform. It is to improve experience for the child, for the family, for the entire ecosystem of support. This requires a fundamental shift in mindset: from isolated services to connected systems, from reactive care to proactive support.

Isolated Services → Connected Systems

Every provider, every setting, every insight unified into one coherent journey for the child.

Reactive Care → Proactive Support

Anticipate needs before they become crises. Act early, act together, act with clarity.

Effort → Flow

When the pieces come together, support transforms from exhausting coordination into natural, seamless care.

> A journey does not become easier because there are more pieces. It becomes easier when the pieces come together. And when they do, support transforms from effort... to flow.

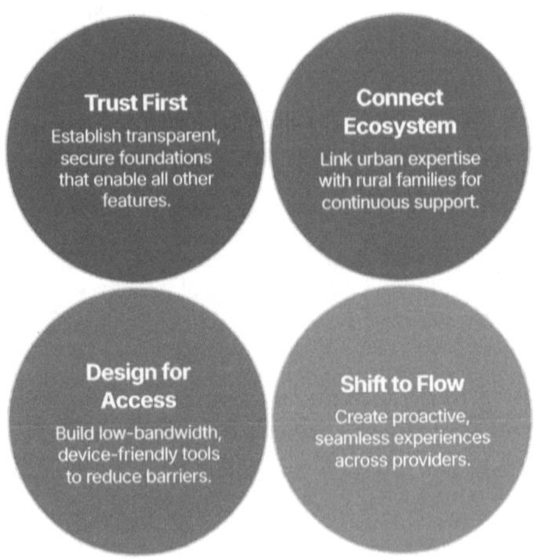

Chapter 33

The Future of Autism Care

We stand at a threshold not just of understanding autism but also of **reimagining how we support it.** From awareness to intelligent support, this chapter explores the shifts already underway and the world we are building together, step by step.

From Recognition to Design

The journey so far has been about recognition, seeing differences, naming needs, and identifying gaps. But the future is not about recognizing problems. It is about **designing solutions**: intentional, integrated, and human-centered.

1

Recognize

Differences, needs, and gaps in existing systems

2

Understand

Context, lived experience, and what support truly means

3

Design

Intentional, inclusive solutions built around the individual

This is the shift from passive awareness to active, purposeful creation of a world that works for everyone.

A World That Adapts Not Demands

For too long, the expectation has been clear: *the individual must adapt to the system.* Learn faster. Fit better. Adjust more. The future may reverse this entirely.

Systems Adapt

Environments and processes reshape themselves to fit individual needs

Environments Respond

Spaces become sensory-aware, flexible, and genuinely welcoming

Learning Flexes

Education moves at the individual's rhythm not a fixed, universal pace

Flexibility becomes the norm not the exception.

Early Understanding & Continuous Support

Early Understanding

One of the most powerful shifts lies in **reducing time between concern and clarity**. Better screening tools, growing awareness, and technology-assisted identification mean families no longer wait years for answers.

- Better screening tools
- Increased community awareness
- Technology-assisted identification

Continuous Support

Today, support often happens in fragments a session here, an intervention there. The future moves toward **continuity**: support that doesn't pause when the session ends.

- Integrated across home, school, and therapy
- Available across all environments
- Responsive in real time

Personalization at the Core

No two individuals are the same yet systems often treat them as if they are. The future moves decisively toward personalization, where support is shaped by the individual, not the average.

Learning Adapts

Curricula and content shift to match each learner's unique strengths, pace, and style

Therapy Evolves

Interventions adjust over time based on real progress and changing needs

Support Responds

Systems recognize the individual in real time, not through a generalized template

Dignity Is Central

Every decision honors the person their identity, voice, and lived experience

The Role of Technology

Technology will continue to expand its role not just as tools, but as **enablers of insight, connection, and accessibility**. AI, digital platforms, and connected systems will work together to reduce fragmentation and improve outcomes. But always as *support* never replacement.

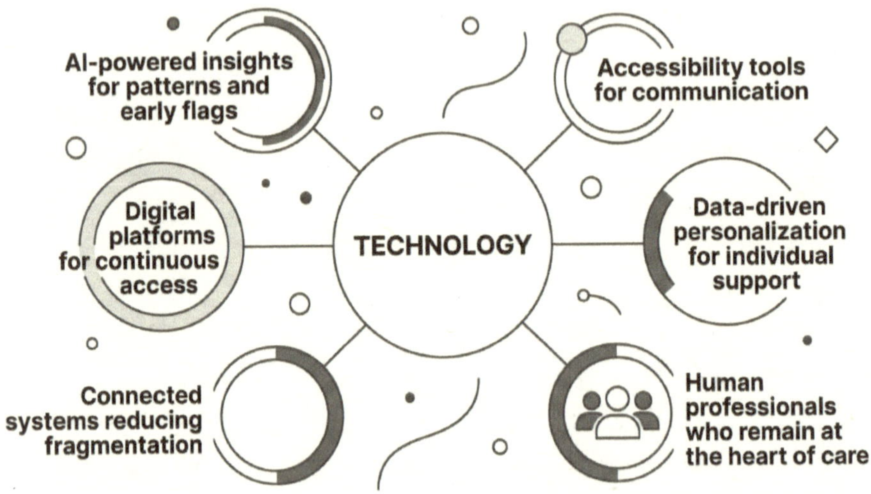

> ⓘ The most powerful technology is the kind that makes human connection easier not the kind that replaces it.

Human Connection Remains Central

> Even in a technologically advanced future, one thing does not change the need for human connection.

What Technology Can Do

- Surface patterns and insights
- Extend access to resources
- Reduce administrative burden
- Enable real-time responsiveness

What Humans Provide

- A parent's unwavering presence
- A teacher's patient guidance
- A therapist's deep empathy
- Understanding that is genuinely felt

Technology may assist but the warmth, judgment, and care that transform a child's life remain beautifully, irreplaceably human.

Building the World Together

EDUCATION | EMPLOYMENT | COMMUNITY | POLICY

The future is not one single change it is many shifts happening across every domain of life, each reinforcing the next.

Education Built for Everyone

Inclusion woven in from the start not retrofitted. Flexible teaching, diverse learning pathways, and support structures that benefit all students.

Workplaces That Value Difference

Role-based hiring, neurodiverse-friendly environments, and recognition that different minds bring different and essential — strengths.

Communities That Understand

Awareness deepening through exposure and experience more accepting, more patient, more genuinely inclusive at every level.

India's Moment of Opportunity

Scale and accessibility remain challenges but technology-driven solutions, a growing ecosystem, and increasing policy focus make the direction genuinely promising.

> The future is not something that arrives. It is something we build step by step, decision by decision. And when built with intention, it becomes not just advanced but **inclusive**.

Chapter 34

For Parents: A Step-by-Step Guide Through the Journey

There is no manual handed to a parent the day this journey begins. No clear map. No perfect sequence. No certainty, only questions. And somewhere beneath those questions, a quiet hope: *Tell me where to begin.* This guide is for you. Twelve steps, one at a time.

Step 1: Observe Without Fear

The journey often begins with noticing a delayed response, a repetitive behavior, or a communication difference. Do not panic. But do not ignore. Observation is not negativity. It is awareness, and awareness is the first act of care.

What to Write Down

- What you notice in your child's behavior
- When the behavior happens
- How often it appears

Patterns matter. A log even a simple one becomes a powerful tool when you speak with professionals.

Observation is the quiet act of showing up. It does not mean something is wrong. It means you are paying attention and that matters deeply.

Steps 2 & 3: Seek Evaluation and Allow Yourself to Feel

Step 2: Seek Evaluation Early

If concerns continue, seek professional guidance not because a label defines your child, but because understanding creates direction. Early evaluation opens doors to clarity, guidance, and access to support. Waiting rarely reduces uncertainty. Understanding does.

Step 3: Emotions Are Part of the Journey

Shock. Fear. Confusion. Denial. These emotions are completely normal. You do not need to feel "strong" immediately. Acceptance is not a single moment it is a process. Give yourself full permission to move through it at your own pace.

Seeking help early is one of the most powerful things a parent can do. It is an act of love, not alarm.

Step 4: Build a Support Team

Support is not one therapist. It is an ecosystem a network of people who understand your child and work together toward shared goals. And at the center of that ecosystem is you.

Speech Therapists

Support communication development, language, and social interaction skills.

Occupational Therapists

Address sensory needs, fine motor skills, and daily living independence.

Teachers & Educators

Shape daily learning environments and academic engagement with your child.

Family Members

Consistency at home is one of the deepest drivers of lasting progress.

Steps 5 & 6: Communication First Structure at Home

Step 5: Focus on Communication

One of the most important goals is **communication,** not perfect speech. A gesture, a word, a visual cue. The ability to express needs changes daily life significantly. Every small step forward deserves to be celebrated, no matter how it looks.

> ✓ Celebrate every step. Progress is progress, regardless of size.

Step 6: Create Structure at Home

Predictability reduces anxiety. Simple, consistent routines provide a sense of safety and safety supports learning. Structure does not mean rigidity; it means creating a dependable rhythm your child can trust.

- Morning routines
- Consistent mealtimes
- Regular sleep schedules

Steps 7 & 8: Sensory World & Letting Go of Comparison

🔊 Overwhelmed by Input

Some children are sensitive to noise, bright lights, or certain textures. What looks like "behavior" may actually be discomfort. Understanding sensory triggers changes how you respond and how your child feels heard.

🌀 Seeking Sensory Input

Others actively seek sensory experiences spinning, touching, moving. This is a way of regulating, not misbehaving. Learning your child's sensory world is a form of deep listening.

📊 Stop Comparing

Every child develops differently. Progress may be slower in some areas and faster in others. Comparison creates unnecessary pain. Focus on **growth, not timelines** your child's story is their own.

> What looks like "behavior" may actually be discomfort. What looks like "delay" may actually be a different timeline. See your child not the comparison.

Steps 9 & 10: Partner With Schools and Care for Yourself

Step 9: Work With Schools

Education works best when collaboration exists. Share your child's triggers, strengths, and what strategies work at home. Teachers cannot support what they do not understand. You are not asking for favors you are building a partnership that benefits your child every single day.

- Share effective strategies from home
- Ask about IEP or 504 plans
- Stay in regular communication

Step 10: Take Care of Yourself

Parents often place themselves last. But burnout helps no one. Rest is not weakness. Seeking support is not failure. You do not need to carry everything alone and the more you care for yourself, the more you can genuinely show up for your child.

> ⓘ You matter in this journey too. Your wellbeing is part of your child's support system.

Steps 11 & 12: Prepare for the Long Journey Hold Onto Possibility

Autism is not a short phase. The journey evolves from childhood to adolescence to adulthood. You do not need to solve the entire future today. Focus on the next step, then the next.

Step 11: One Step at a Time

The journey ahead is long and that is okay. Do not carry tomorrow's weight today. Progress unfolds in seasons. Trust the process, and stay grounded in what is possible right now.

Step 12: Hold Onto Possibility

The future may look different than expected. But different does not mean hopeless. Growth happens. Connection happens. Progress happens sometimes slowly, sometimes unexpectedly. But it happens.

> **You do not need to know everything to move forward. You only need to begin and continue.**

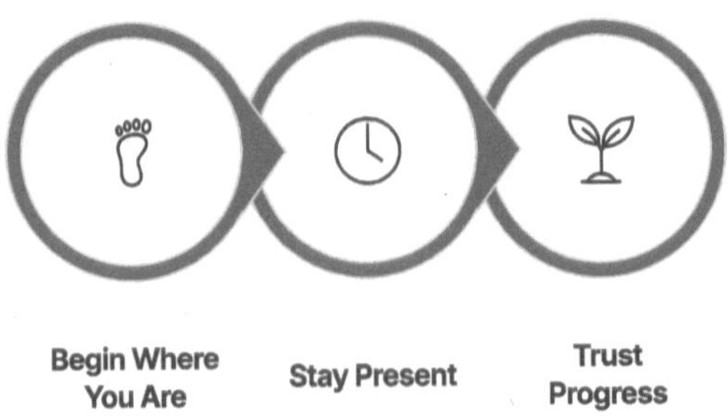

You will make mistakes. You will feel uncertain. You will have difficult days. And still your presence, consistency, and love remain one of the most powerful supports in your child's life.

Chapter 35

Teaching Beyond the Curriculum

There is a moment every educator experiences. A child sits in the classroom present but disconnected. The lesson continues, instructions are given, and yet something is not reaching the child. Not because the child cannot learn. But because learning is not happening in the way the system expects. This chapter is for every educator who has felt that gap and wants to close it.

Education Is Not Just Delivery of Content

For many years, education has been designed around standardization. Same curriculum. Same pace. Same expectations. This approach works for many students but autism challenges a deeper assumption: that all minds learn in the same way.

They do not. And perhaps they were never meant to. When we design classrooms only for the "average" learner, we inadvertently build walls around those who think, process, and engage with the world differently.

> The classroom was built for one kind of mind. It's time to redesign it for all minds.

The Core Shift

From standardization → to differentiation

From one pace → to flexible pacing

From uniform outcomes → to individual progress

From compliance → to understanding

From "Problem Child" to "Different Learner"

One of the most important transformations in inclusive education begins not in the classroom but in perception. The way an educator sees a child shapes every interaction that follows.

What We See	What It May Mean	What Changes With Reframing
• Avoids eye contact • Struggles with transitions • Reacts strongly to noise • Refuses instructions	• Processing differences • Need for predictability • Sensory sensitivity • Anxiety or overwhelm	• Curiosity replaces frustration • Support replaces punishment • Connection replaces conflict • Progress becomes possible

Understanding this distinction changes the entire classroom dynamic and opens the door to genuine learning.

Safety, Structure, and Communication

A child cannot learn effectively under constant stress. Emotional safety must come before academic instruction. When these three foundational supports are in place, engagement improves naturally and deeply.

Learning Begins With Safety

- Predictable daily routines
- Calm, steady communication
- Reduced sensory overload

Structure Supports Learning

- Visual schedules on display
- Step-by-step guidance
- Clear transitions between tasks

Flexible Communication

- Allow more processing time
- Offer visual instructions
- Avoid open-ended verbal prompts

> These are not special privileges. They are learning supports and they benefit many students, not just those with autism.

Behavior Is Often Communication

When a Child...

- Walks away from a task
- Refuses to do work
- Reacts emotionally or intensely
- Shuts down or melts down

...they are not necessarily misbehaving.

Ask Instead:

What is this child trying to tell me? The behavior may reflect anxiety, sensory overload, or genuine difficulty understanding the task.

Responding with **curiosity instead of punishment** shifts outcomes dramatically. It transforms a discipline moment into a teaching moment and a child who felt judged begins to feel understood.

> Every behavior is a message. Our job is to decode it, not suppress it.

Strength-Based Learning & True Inclusion

Many autistic students possess remarkable strengths. Education should not focus only on deficits it must also identify and nurture what students do well. Because confidence grows through competence.

Pattern Recognition

Exceptional ability to identify patterns, sequences, and systems

Remarkable Memory

Strong recall for facts, routines, and areas of deep interest

Detail Orientation

Noticing nuances others miss, with precision and accuracy

Deep Focus

Sustained engagement and expertise in areas of personal interest

True inclusion means ensuring the child can participate, learn, and feel accepted not just physically occupy a seat in the room.

The Ecosystem of Support

No educator succeeds alone. Inclusive education requires a web of support from peers in the classroom to parents at home, from institutional systems to individual teachers committed to growth.

Peers and Classroom Culture

When educators foster empathy, patience, and respect for differences, peer acceptance improves naturally. Students learn from each other and social belonging becomes possible. Culture is shaped by what is modeled and what is celebrated.

Collaboration With Parents

Parents carry deep insight into their child what works at home, what triggers stress, what supports regulation. When schools and families collaborate, support becomes consistent across environments. And consistency strengthens progress for everyone.

Educator Wellbeing & Training

Teaching neurodiverse learners in large classrooms with limited support is genuinely demanding. Educators who feel underprepared or overwhelmed need institutional backing training, resources, and space to grow without judgment.

What Great Educators Do Differently

Great educators often do one thing exceptionally well: **they see the child before the challenge.** A calmer response. A flexible approach. A moment of genuine understanding. These moments stay with students far longer than any lesson plan.

See the Whole Child

Look beyond behaviors to the person their strengths, their story, their needs

Adapt With Intention

Adjust environment, pacing, and communication before expecting the child to adjust

Build Consistent Partnerships

Collaborate with parents and specialists to create unified, coherent support

Choose Understanding Over Judgment

Respond to difficulty with curiosity and transform discipline into connection

> Education is not only about teaching information. It is about creating environments where learning becomes possible. And sometimes, the most powerful change in a child's journey begins with one educator who chose understanding over judgment.

Chapter 36

For Policymakers Designing Systems That Truly Support

There is a point where individual effort is no longer enough. A parent can try. A teacher can adapt. A therapist can guide. But when systems remain fragmented, progress becomes dependent on persistence rather than accessibility. **That is where policy matters.**

Policy Is Not Abstract

Policies are often seen as documents frameworks, regulations, and announcements. But for families navigating autism support, policy becomes real in everyday life. It shapes what is possible and what remains out of reach.

Accessibility

Whether support is reachable for all families, regardless of income or location

Inclusion

Whether schools are genuinely structured to welcome and educate every child

Affordability

Whether therapies and services are financially accessible without hardship

Adulthood

Whether support continues meaningfully beyond childhood into adult life

> Policy shapes lived experience. Every framework written in an office is felt in a family's daily reality.

The Current Reality Fragmented Support

Most autism ecosystems today operate in silos. Healthcare functions separately from education. Education functions separately from employment support. Therapies function separately from community systems. The result is that **families become the coordinators** navigating disconnected structures continuously, at significant personal cost.

What Families Face

- Repeated referrals between unconnected providers
- Loss of information at every transition
- Time and energy spent bridging systemic gaps
- No single point of continuity or coordination

What Systems Should Provide

- Coordinated pathways from diagnosis onward
- Shared information across departments
- Reduced administrative burden on caregivers
- Consistent, trackable developmental support

The Burden Should Not Fall on Families Alone

A family caring for an autistic child already carries enormous weight emotional responsibility, financial pressure, and the daily demands of caregiving. They should not also carry the burden of fixing the system that is supposed to support them. Systems must be designed to **reduce burden, not increase it.**

Emotional Load

Caregivers navigate grief, advocacy, and daily decision-making simultaneously often without adequate support themselves.

Financial Pressure

Therapies, assessments, and specialized education carry significant costs that most families manage without adequate public support.

Daily Caregiving

Routines, appointments, school coordination, and behavioral support require continuous, sustained effort every single day.

Good policy design asks: does this system reduce or increase the weight families carry? That question should guide every decision.

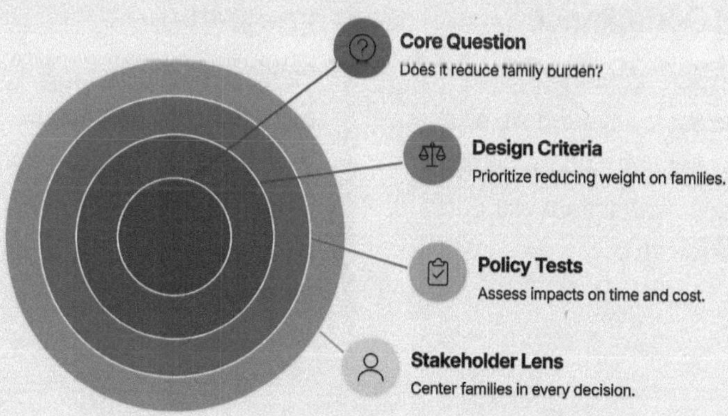

Core Principles for Accessible, Equitable Systems

Building systems that truly support autism requires more than intent it requires structural commitment across several foundational principles. Each principle addresses a specific gap that currently leaves families behind.

Early Support Must Be Accessible

Early intervention changes trajectories. Policy must prioritize early screening, community-level awareness, and affordable intervention because timing matters deeply.

Urban Access Cannot Be the Only Model

In many countries, including India, support concentrates in urban centers. But autism exists everywhere. Systems must extend into smaller towns, rural communities, and underserved populations.

Education Must Evolve Beyond Compliance

True inclusion requires teacher training, classroom support, and individualized learning pathways not symbolic enrollment without structural backing.

Healthcare Must Become Integrated

Families should not move between disconnected providers repeatedly. Integration connects diagnosis, therapy, education, and developmental tracking into continuous care.

The Missing Focus: Supporting the Full Lifecycle

Most systems invest heavily in early childhood support and rightly so. But autism is lifelong. The absence of robust policy for adulthood leaves individuals and families without a path forward precisely when they need one most. **Policy must support the full lifecycle.**

What Adulthood Requires

- Employment pathways and workplace inclusion frameworks
- Independent and supported living options
- Long-term care and community integration models
- Continuity of support as families age

Without these, the progress achieved in childhood has nowhere to land.

The Economics Cannot Be Ignored

Without policy intervention, care becomes dependent on financial capacity creating deep inequality. Insurance inclusion, public programs, and subsidized models must be part of any serious policy framework.

What Systemic Change Actually Requires

Redesigning support ecosystems demands coordinated action across multiple domains simultaneously. No single department or ministry can address this alone which is precisely why cross-ministerial coordination is essential.

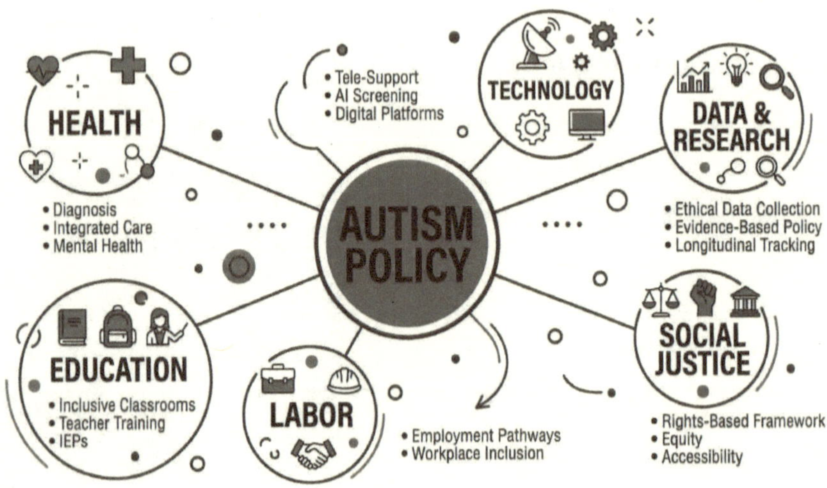

Autism intersects with health, education, labor, social justice, technology, and research. Effective policy must reflect that interconnection not assign responsibility to a single department operating in isolation.

A Rights-Based Vision for the Future

The future of autism support should not depend on whether a family is financially privileged, geographically connected, or system-savvy. Support must be structured, scalable, and accessible by design not by luck.

1 **Charity**

Support given when convenient

2 **Programs**

Structured services for some

3 **Systems**

Coordinated, integrated ecosystems

4 **Rights**

Dignity, inclusion, and access as guarantees

> The effectiveness of a society is also measured by how well it supports those who experience the world differently. **Good policy does not simply create systems it creates possibility.**

When systems are designed with humanity at the center, support becomes not accidental but **dependable**. That is the standard policymakers have the power and responsibility to meet.

Chapter 37

Building Solutions That Truly Matter

For Startups and Innovators

Autism is not only a healthcare challenge; it is a systems challenge. And wherever systems struggle, innovation begins to emerge. This chapter is a call to builders, founders, and designers who want to create something genuinely meaningful in one of the most human, complex, and underserved ecosystems in the world.

The Problem Is Not the Absence of Effort

Today, countless families are trying. Parents are learning. Teachers are adapting. Therapists are supporting. And yet, gaps remain not because people do not care, but because the ecosystem itself is deeply fragmented.

This is where innovators often see opportunity. But autism is not a space that needs "disruption" alone. It needs understanding. The gap is not a lack of willingness it is a lack of connection between the many moving parts of support.

The Real Challenge

- → Fragmented systems
- → Disconnected stakeholders
- → Uncoordinated care

Human Problems Cannot Be Solved Only Technically

Many startups begin with technology an app, a platform, an AI engine. But autism support is deeply human. Which means successful innovation requires more than technical capability.

Empathy

Understanding the emotional landscape of families living with autism every single day.

Observation

Watching, listening, and learning before designing. Real insight comes from proximity.

Long-Term Thinking

Autism support is a lifelong journey. Solutions must serve families across years, not just moments.

The First Mistake: Building Without Listening

One of the most common mistakes innovators make is solving what they *assume* is the problem without deeply understanding lived experience.

⚠ What builders often provide

- More data dashboards
- More notifications and alerts
- More feature complexity

✓ What families actually need

- Simplicity and clarity
- Reduced daily stress
- Trustworthy guidance

The real challenge is not always technological it is experiential. Builders who spend time with families before writing a single line of code will always outperform those who don't.

The Opportunity Is Massive but Sensitive

The autism ecosystem contains enormous unmet needs. This creates significant innovation potential but it is also a sensitive space, because families are vulnerable to false promises and overstated claims.

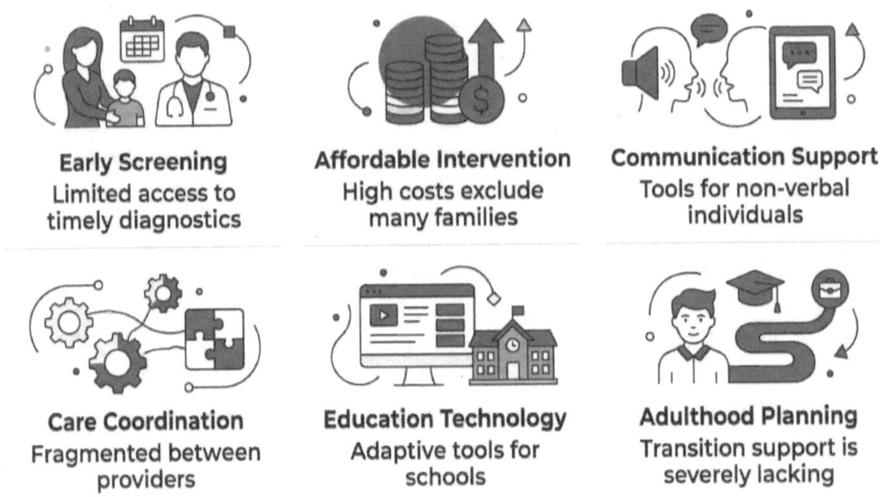

Designing for Real Life

Solutions must work in reality not just in demonstrations. A platform that succeeds in ideal conditions may fail completely in daily family life.

Too Complex

Cognitive overload kills adoption for already-stressed caregivers.

Too Expensive

Cost barriers exclude the families who need support most.

Too Time-Consuming

Tools that demand more time add burden rather than reduce it.

> The best solutions reduce burden. Not increase it.

Affordability Is Innovation Too

In many parts of the world particularly in countries like India affordability is not a secondary concern. It is the central one. A highly advanced solution that reaches only a few families does not solve the broader challenge.

True scale means designing for inclusion from day one. Not as an afterthought.

True scale is inclusion.

1. **Lower cost**

   Drive down price through smart design and technology leverage

2. **Expand access**

   Reach underserved geographies and communities

3. **Simplify delivery**

   Make onboarding effortless for all literacy levels

Technology Should Enhance Human Systems

The goal is not to replace therapists, teachers, or parents. It is to support them. The most effective technology quietly removes friction from the lives of the humans doing the real work.

Reduce Repetitive Burden

Automate documentation, progress notes, and scheduling so professionals spend time with people not paperwork.

Improve Continuity

Ensure insights from therapy carry meaningfully into school and home environments without friction.

Enhance Understanding

Give parents, teachers, and therapists clearer windows into what a child is experiencing and progressing through.

AI Can Transform the Ecosystem If Used Responsibly

Artificial Intelligence offers enormous possibilities for autism support from early pattern detection to personalized learning pathways. But the power of AI in this space is matched only by its responsibility.

What AI Can Do

- Detect early developmental patterns
- Personalize learning experiences
- Power predictive support systems

What AI Must Always Be

- Transparent in its reasoning
- Ethical in data use
- Human-centered in design

> Children are not datasets. And behavior is not merely data.

The Need for Integrated Platforms

One of the biggest opportunities in autism innovation lies in integration. Today, schools work separately from therapists, therapists work separately from parents, and data remains fragmented across systems that never speak to each other.

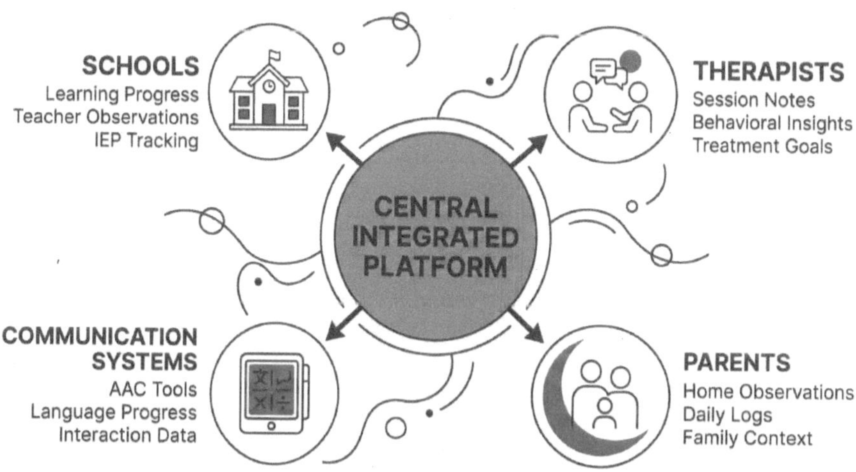

An integrated platform could create continuity across every environment a child inhabits — transforming disconnected data points into a coherent, living picture of development.

Innovation Requires Multidisciplinary Thinking

Autism solutions cannot be built by technology teams alone. The strongest systems emerge when multiple perspectives align from the very beginning of the design process — not as an afterthought.

Psychologists

Educators

Therapists

Designers

Families

Engineers

The Risk of "Optimization Thinking"

The Danger

Treating autism support purely as an optimization problem leads to solutions that maximize outputs but minimize humanity.

There is a subtle but serious danger in applying pure optimization logic to human development. The impulse to maximize outputs, normalize behavior, or standardize responses feels productive — but it misses something essential.

Human development is not software optimization. Every individual develops differently, on their own timeline, with their own strengths. Innovation must respect — and celebrate — that individuality rather than engineer it away.

> The most dangerous innovation is one that works perfectly on average but fails the individual in front of you.

What Families Actually Value

Most families are not looking for perfection. They are not seeking the most advanced system or the most feature-rich platform. They are looking for something that genuinely eases the weight of daily life.

Practicality

Does it fit into an already full day? Can a tired parent use it at 9pm without frustration?

Reliability

Does it work consistently? Can families depend on it when it matters most?

Emotional Ease

Does it reduce stress or add to it? Does it feel like support or another obligation?

Trustworthiness

Does it keep its promises? Is it honest about what it can and cannot do?

Building With Responsibility

Innovation in autism carries responsibility that extends far beyond product metrics. When a solution succeeds or fails, the impact is not measured in downloads or revenue — it is measured in childhood experiences, family well-being, and long-term independence.

This is not just a market. It is a human ecosystem. Builders who enter this space carry a genuine duty of care to the families who will trust them with some of the most important moments of their lives.

Childhood Experiences

Family Well-Being

Long-Term Independence

A Vision for the Future

The future of autism support is not a distant dream — it is a design challenge. The technology exists. The will exists. What is needed now is intentional, empathy-led, responsibly executed innovation.

1. Accessible Early Support

Screening and intervention available everywhere, not just in major cities.

2. Clearly Guided Parents

Families navigating with confidence, not confusion.

3. Intelligently Adaptive Schools

Education systems that flex to meet every learner's unique needs.

4. Ethical AI Assistance

Technology that amplifies human judgment rather than replacing it.

5. Seamlessly Connected Systems

A unified ecosystem where every stakeholder moves in the same direction.

A Final Reflection for Innovators

> The most meaningful innovations are not those that simply scale technology. They are the ones that scale understanding.

In autism support, success is not measured only by intelligence. It is measured by impact on human lives. The builders who will shape this ecosystem are not necessarily those with the most advanced AI or the largest funding rounds.

They are the ones who sit with families. Who listen before they build. Who measure impact in moments of relief, clarity, and connection — not in vanity metrics.

When innovation is guided by empathy, technology becomes not just powerful but **transformative.**

Listen First

Understand lived experience before writing a single line of code.

Design for Reality

Build for Tuesday evening, not the product demo.

Measure What Matters

Count moments of genuine human impact, not just engagement metrics.

Chapter 38

The Holistic Autism Framework

From Isolated Interventions to Connected Support

There is a pattern that repeats across the autism journey. A child receives therapy. A school tries to adapt. A parent learns through experience. Each effort is meaningful. Each effort valuable. And yet, something still feels incomplete because the challenge is not always the absence of support. **It is the absence of connection between supports.**

The Problem Is Fragmentation

Today, most autism ecosystems operate in parts. Healthcare functions separately. Education functions separately. Therapy functions separately. And families move constantly between them carrying information, repeating stories, and trying to create continuity where systems do not.

The child experiences **one life.** But the system responds in **fragments.**

> A deeper question is needed: *How do we connect the entire journey into one coherent system?*

Questions We've Been Asking

- Which therapy works best?
- Which school is suitable?
- Which intervention should begin first?

The Question We Need

How do we **connect the entire journey** into one coherent system?

What Is a Holistic Autism Framework?

A holistic framework does not focus on one intervention alone. It recognizes that autism touches **multiple dimensions simultaneously** which means support must also be multidimensional.

Communication

Supporting expressive and receptive language across all environments.

Learning

Adapting education to individual strengths and learning styles.

Sensory Processing

Understanding and reducing sensory overwhelm in daily life.

Emotional Development

Building emotional regulation and resilience over time.

Family Dynamics

Aligning the home environment with therapeutic goals.

Long-Term Independence

Planning pathways toward meaningful adult participation.

The Four Layers of the Framework

A truly holistic system can be understood through **four connected layers** each one essential, each one reinforcing the others.

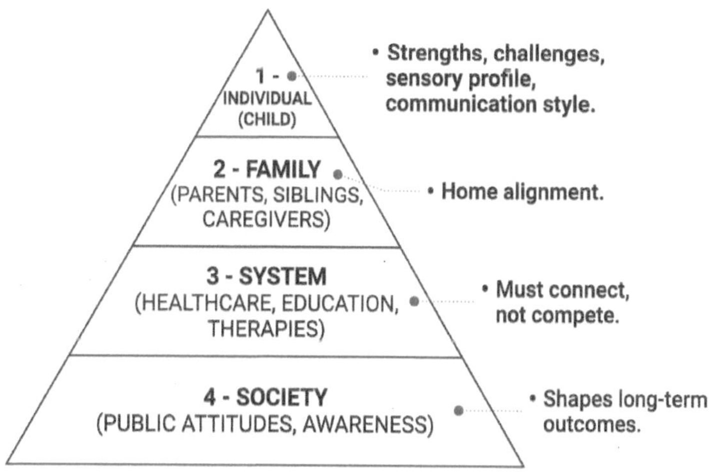

Support begins with the individual but cannot succeed without the family, the formal system, and ultimately a more inclusive society. Each layer shapes the one within it.

The Child Is Not the Problem to Solve

One of the most important shifts in this framework is **philosophical**. The goal is not to "normalize" the individual. This changes the tone of the entire ecosystem.

Support Functioning

Build on what the individual already does well.

Reduce Distress

Remove unnecessary barriers that create struggle.

Increase Participation

Enable meaningful engagement in community life.

Enable Dignity

Honor identity while expanding independence.

From Reactive to Predictive Support

How Most Systems Work Today

A meltdown happens

Then a response is created.

A school issue emerges

Then adjustments are made.

A developmental gap widens

Then a new referral begins.

How a Holistic System Moves

Early Identification

Recognize patterns before challenges escalate.

Continuous Monitoring

Track progress across all environments consistently.

Adaptive Intervention

Adjust support as the individual grows and changes.

Not to control the child but to **reduce struggle before it intensifies.** Predictive support respects the individual's journey while staying one step ahead of barriers.

Continuity, Technology & AI

Support should not reset every time the environment changes. A child should not have to re-explain needs, restart adaptation, or rebuild understanding repeatedly. **Continuity means information flows, strategies align, and support evolves consistently.**

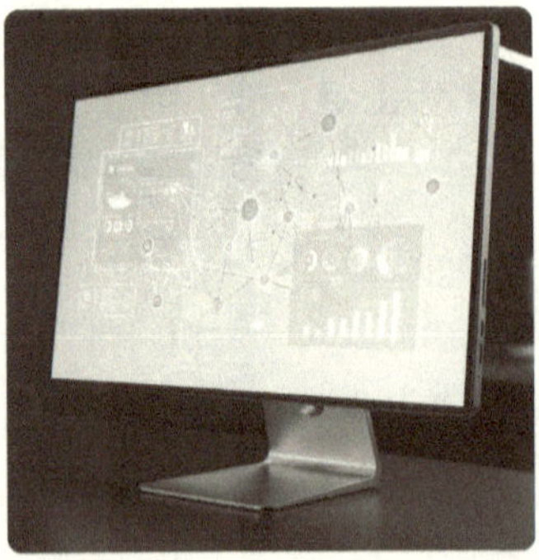

Technology as a Connector

Integrated platforms can connect therapists, schools, families, and healthcare providers creating one evolving support ecosystem. Not through complexity. Through continuity.

The Role of AI

AI can strengthen the framework through pattern recognition, personalized learning, and predictive support insights. But AI must remain ethical, transparent, and human-guided because intelligence without empathy creates efficient but incomplete systems.

A Vision Worth Building

The future of autism support will not be defined only by better therapies. It will be defined by **better integration**. This is not impossible. It is a design challenge and one that India, with its evolving systems, is uniquely positioned to lead.

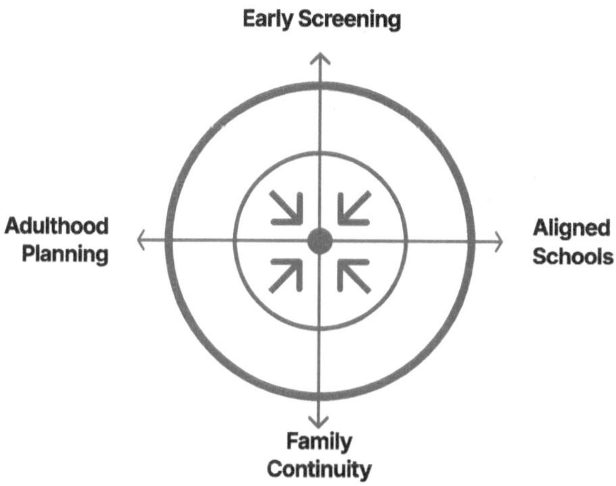

A fragmented system asks families to carry the burden alone. An integrated system **carries the journey with them**. When support becomes connected, possibility expands not only for the individual, but for society itself.

> Autism support is not a single service. **It is an ecosystem.**

This framework moves the conversation beyond therapy toward infrastructure, coordination, lifecycle planning, and long-term inclusion.

Chapter 39

India Blueprint: What Needs to Change

There is a moment when awareness alone is no longer enough. Conversations increase. Policies emerge. Institutions begin to respond. And yet, families still struggle not because progress is absent, but because progress remains uneven. This chapter examines the interconnected challenges shaping India's autism ecosystem and the coordinated transformation it urgently requires.

A Country of Contrasts

India is a country of immense capability. Advanced hospitals exist alongside underserved communities. World-class technology exists alongside limited accessibility. Awareness is growing rapidly yet silence still remains in many places.

This contrast defines the autism ecosystem as well. Some families access support early. Others spend years searching for answers. The gap between what is possible and what is accessible is the central challenge this blueprint seeks to address.

The Reality Today

Urban Centers

Specialist access, early diagnosis, structured therapy pathways

Smaller Towns

Limited expertise, long wait times, fragmented services

Rural Areas

Minimal awareness, no screening, families searching alone

Not One Problem Many Connected Problems

Autism support in India is not limited by a single gap. It is shaped by multiple interconnected realities that reinforce each other. Addressing any one in isolation leaves the others unresolved.

Late Identification

Signs missed or dismissed

Limited Specialist Access

Concentrated in cities

Uneven Education

Inclusion in name only

Financial Burden

Unaffordable long-term care

Social Stigma

Judgment and misunderstanding

Fragmented Services

Siloed systems, no coordination

These issues do not exist separately they reinforce each other. A coordinated response is not optional; it is essential.

The First Need: Early Awareness at Scale

Many families still encounter autism late not because signs were absent, but because awareness was limited. Parents are frequently told to "wait, the child will improve," or "boys speak late," or "it is just a phase." These dismissals delay recognition, and delays in recognition delay intervention.

Awareness must move beyond cities and into the systems that families already trust and use every day.

> "Every month of delayed identification is a month of missed opportunity for early intervention."

Where Awareness Must Reach

→ **Primary Healthcare Systems**

Pediatricians and family doctors as first points of screening

→ **Community Health Workers**

ASHA workers and Anganwadi centers trained in early signs

→ **Schools**

Teachers equipped to recognize and refer appropriately

→ **Rural Networks**

Grassroots reach into underserved communities

Diagnosis Should Not Depend on Geography

Today, access to specialists is concentrated in urban areas. Families in smaller towns face long travel distances, delayed appointments, and limited expertise creating a profound inequality in who receives timely diagnosis and who does not.

Tele-Assessment Support

Connecting families in remote areas with qualified specialists through secure digital platforms reducing the need for costly travel.

Remote Guidance Systems

Structured remote protocols that guide local health workers through developmental screening processes with specialist oversight.

Hybrid Care Models

Combining in-person community touchpoints with digital follow-up to create continuous, accessible support pathways.

ⓘ Technology can bridge the geographic gap but infrastructure investment and policy support are equally essential to make these models sustainable at scale.

Education Requires Structural Reform

Inclusive education cannot succeed through policy statements alone. Without structural change at the classroom level, inclusion becomes symbolic rather than functional. The gap between stated policy and daily classroom reality remains significant across India's education system.

What Schools Need

Teacher Training

Ongoing, practical training in neurodiversity and classroom adaptation

Classroom Adaptation Tools

Visual supports, sensory accommodations, structured routines

Special Educator Support

Dedicated resource persons within school structures

Flexible Evaluation

Assessment systems that reflect diverse learning profiles

The Teacher Gap

Many educators genuinely want to help but they often lack training, resources, and system support. A sustainable model must support teachers alongside students. Overwhelmed educators cannot deliver inclusive outcomes consistently, regardless of intent.

⚠ Without investing in teacher capacity, every inclusive education policy risks remaining a promise rather than a practice.

Therapy Access and the Missing Focus: Adulthood

Making Therapy Accessible

Therapy access remains deeply unequal. Cost, urban concentration, and long-term affordability place consistent support out of reach for most families. India requires scalable models that bring support closer to families not limited to specialized urban centers.

Clinical Expertise

Specialist knowledge anchoring quality

Community Delivery

Trained local practitioners extending reach

Technology-Enabled Continuity

Digital tools bridging gaps between sessions

The Adulthood Gap

One of the largest gaps in India's autism ecosystem is adulthood planning. Most support systems focus on childhood. Far fewer address what comes next leaving families navigating uncertainty alone, especially as parents age.

Employment Pathways

Structured vocational programs and employer partnerships

Independent Living

Supported housing and daily living skills programs

Long-Term Social Inclusion

Community belonging beyond school years

Policy Exists But Integration Is Weak

India has made important progress through disability rights frameworks, inclusive education policies, and certification systems. But systems still function in silos. Healthcare, education, employment, and social welfare each operate separately and families become the exhausted coordinators between them.

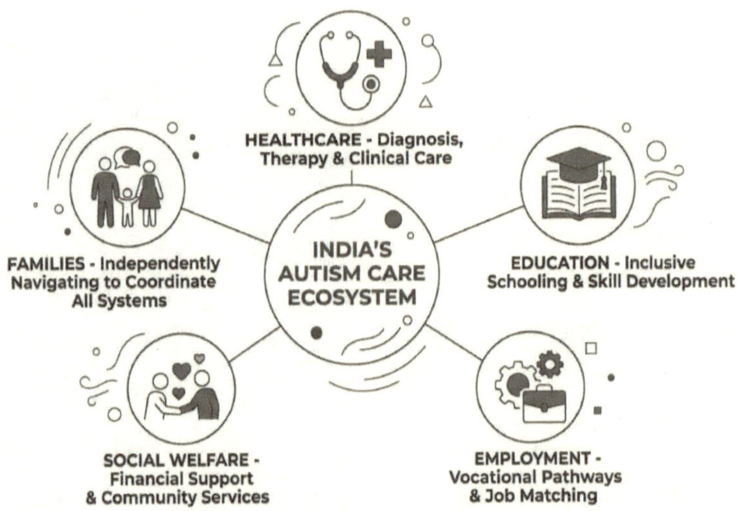

⚠ When families bear the coordination burden between siloed systems, the most vulnerable families those with fewest resources are most likely to fall through the cracks entirely.

The Need for a National Autism Framework

India needs more than isolated programs. It needs a coordinated national framework that connects every stage of the autism journey from the earliest screening through to adult life planning across the full lifecycle and across the full geography of the country.

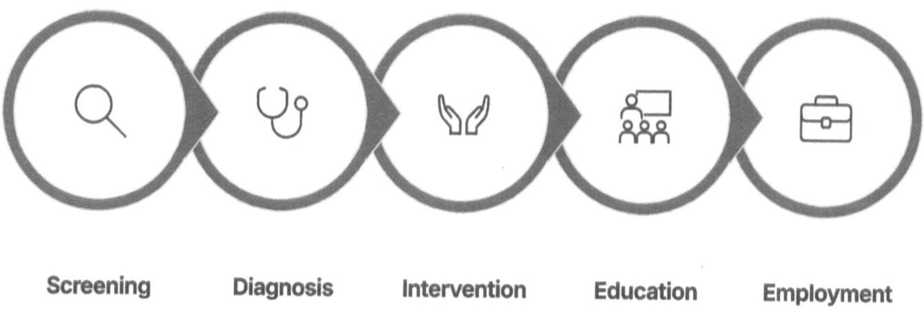

This connected lifecycle approach ensures that no family reaches a dead end at any stage. Each system feeds into the next, reducing the burden on families to find and coordinate their own pathways through fragmented services.

The Role of Technology and AI

India has a unique opportunity because it is simultaneously digitally expanding, demographically large, and resource-constrained. This combination means that well-designed technology can achieve what additional infrastructure alone cannot: extending quality support into underserved regions at scale.

AI and digital systems can reduce specialist dependency, improve continuity of care, and bring support closer to families who currently have none. But technology must be designed with three non-negotiable principles.

Affordable

Designed for diverse income groups, not premium markets

Ethical

Transparent, accountable, and free from harmful bias

Human-Centered

Technology that augments human care never replaces it

ⓘ India's digital expansion is an asset but only if technology solutions are designed from the ground up for accessibility, affordability, and the realities of low-resource environments.

Community, NGOs, and Changing Mindsets

NGOs as System Multipliers

India's NGO ecosystem has played a critical role in filling gaps where public systems were weak. Long-term sustainability requires deeper collaboration with public systems, standardization of quality, and greater geographic reach transforming NGOs from gap-fillers to system-builders.

Shifting Social Mindsets

Systems alone cannot solve everything. Families still encounter judgment, misunderstanding, and social exclusion. Public awareness must evolve through three stages: from recognition, to acceptance, to genuine inclusion where difference is not merely tolerated but embraced as part of community life.

Affordability at the Core

A support system that only serves privileged families cannot solve the larger challenge. Scalability in India depends entirely on affordability. Every solution must be designed for diverse income groups, rural accessibility, and low-resource environments from the very beginning.

The Vision Ahead

An India built for inclusion

1

Universal Screening

Early screening available in every district, embedded in primary healthcare

2

Equipped Schools

Every school trained, resourced, and structurally ready for inclusive education

3

Accessible Therapy

Affordable, community-delivered, technology-supported therapeutic care

4

Employment Pathways

Structured vocational and employment systems for autistic adults

5

Ethical AI

Technology that extends human care affordably and responsibly

6

Continuous Family Support

Families supported across the full lifecycle not only in childhood

This is not unrealistic. It requires coordinated intent and the will to build systems designed for everyone from the beginning.

A Final Reflection

The question is no longer whether India needs a better autism ecosystem. That answer is clear. The question is how quickly a system that is inclusive, scalable, and sustainable can be built and whether the collective will exists to build it with intention.

> "A nation is ultimately measured not only by economic growth but by how well it supports those who experience the world differently."

When systems are designed with inclusion at their core, development becomes not only faster but also more humane. India is still building many of its future systems. That is not a limitation. It is an opportunity to build them right.

The blueprint exists. The need is documented. The technology is available. What remains is the coordinated commitment across government, institutions, communities, and families to move from awareness to action.

Chapter 40

Global Playbook: What the World Can Learn and Share

Autism is experienced individually but the challenge surrounding it is global. Across countries, cultures, and systems, families ask the same questions: How do we support better? How do we build inclusive systems? How do we prepare for the future? The details may differ, but the underlying journey remains remarkably similar. This chapter explores what the world has learned and what we must build together.

No Country Has Fully Solved the Challenge

Some nations have stronger healthcare systems. Others have advanced educational models. Some lead in technology and research. And yet, no country has fully solved autism support. Why? Because autism is not a single-domain issue it touches every pillar of society simultaneously.

Healthcare

Diagnosis, early intervention, and clinical pathways

Education

Inclusive classrooms and individualized learning

Employment

Workplace access and adult independence

Social Inclusion

Community belonging and public acceptance

Public Policy

Legislation, funding, and systemic frameworks

Technology

AI tools, digital therapeutics, and innovation

Fragmented solutions focused on only one or two of these pillars will always remain incomplete. Lasting progress requires connected, cross-domain systems working in harmony.

The Global Shift: From Awareness to System Design

The world is gradually moving through three pivotal phases in how it understands and responds to autism. Many countries are still transitioning between these phases simultaneously and understanding where a system sits is the first step toward moving it forward.

Phase 1: Awareness

Recognizing that autism exists and that it deserves attention, resources, and a public conversation. The first and most foundational step.

Phase 2: Acceptance

Reducing stigma, increasing inclusion, and affirming that autistic individuals belong fully in their communities, schools, and workplaces.

Phase 3: System Design

Building connected ecosystems that support individuals throughout their entire lives from early childhood through adulthood as a societal responsibility.

What Stronger Systems Have in Common

Despite profound cultural and structural differences, the most successful autism support ecosystems around the world share a set of core principles. The specific models vary but the underlying philosophy remains strikingly similar.

Shared Principles of Success

- Early identification at the community level
- Integrated support systems across sectors
- Inclusive education with real accommodations
- Active family involvement at every stage
- Long-term planning that extends beyond childhood

The Core Insight

No single program or policy creates a strong ecosystem. It is the **integration of principles** working together across health, education, and society — that produces outcomes families can actually depend on.

Countries that treat these principles as a connected framework, rather than isolated initiatives, consistently demonstrate stronger developmental outcomes for autistic individuals.

Early Intervention: A Universal Lesson

Countries with stronger developmental outcomes share one consistent priority: early identification and support. The lesson is universal timing matters more than almost any other variable in a child's trajectory.

Community-Level Screening

Moving identification beyond specialist clinics and into pediatric, community, and school-based settings makes early recognition accessible to all families, regardless of location or income.

Parent Education

Empowering families with knowledge and practical strategies amplifies the impact of professional intervention because parents are present in a child's life every single day.

Early Intervention Access

When support is introduced early, it reduces long-term challenges, improves adaptive functioning, and strengthens communication and learning pathways in ways that become significantly harder later.

> Support introduced early doesn't just help the child it reshapes the entire family's journey.

Education Systems That Adapt

Globally, education systems are recognizing that inclusion requires far more than physical access. Placing a child in a general classroom without structural support is not inclusion it is proximity. The most effective systems around the world have made a fundamental shift in how they frame their mission.

The Old Model	The Emerging Model
"How do we fit the child into the existing classroom?"	"How do we design classrooms that support diverse learners?"
Compliance-focused. Deficit-oriented. Child adapts to the system.	Strengths-focused. Systems adapt. Inclusion is built in, not bolted on.

Effective systems globally invest in **teacher training, flexible learning methods, classroom accommodations,** and **individualized support pathways**. These are not luxuries they are the structural requirements of genuine inclusion.

The Employment Gap: A Global Crisis

Even in the most developed nations, adulthood remains one of the largest unaddressed gaps in autism support. Transition from school does not automatically lead to opportunity and for too many individuals, it leads to isolation instead.

Where the System Falls Short

- Employment access remains disproportionately low
- Workplace environments are rarely designed for neurodiversity
- Independent living pathways are underfunded
- Support often ends at age 18 or 21

⚠ Autism support cannot stop after the school years. A system that invests only in childhood and leaves adulthood unaddressed is structurally incomplete.

What Progress Looks Like

Countries and organizations pioneering change are building structured employment programs, neurodiversity hiring initiatives, job coaching services, and adult day programs with dignity at their center.

The most important shift is philosophical: viewing autistic adults not as recipients of care, but as contributors to society who deserve equitable pathways to participation and independence.

Technology as a Global Equalizer

One of the most transformative developments in autism support globally is the rise of technology. AI, digital therapeutics, and connected platforms have the potential to reach individuals in regions where specialist concentration remains low extending support to families who would otherwise receive none.

Extending Reach

Technology can extend support into underserved and rural regions, reducing the geographic barriers that leave many families without access to any specialized guidance.

Personalizing at Scale

AI-assisted tools can personalize interventions for individual children in ways that were previously only possible through intensive one-on-one specialist time.

The Human Balance

But advanced systems can still fail if they ignore human realities. Families need more than efficient systems they need **trust, simplicity, and emotional understanding.** Technology must serve humanity, not replace it.

> The most successful global models balance technology with humanity not one at the expense of the other.

The Role of Culture Cannot Be Ignored

Autism is experienced within cultural environments. Beliefs about disability, education, independence, and family responsibility shape how support systems evolve and how families experience them. A global playbook that ignores culture will fail the people it intends to serve.

Family Structures

In many cultures, extended family plays a central caregiving role. Support systems that only address the nuclear family miss the broader ecosystem of support already present.

Disability Beliefs

Cultural perceptions of disability vary widely from spiritual interpretations to medical framings. Systems must meet families where they are, not where the framework assumes they should be.

Adaptive Frameworks

Global principles must remain adaptable not rigidly standardized. The goal is to share wisdom, not to impose uniformity onto deeply different communities.

What the World Can Learn From Each Other

A true global playbook is not about copying one country's model. It is about learning collectively recognizing that every nation holds a piece of the answer, and that no single system has them all. The most powerful progress happens when knowledge flows freely across borders.

NORDIC COUNTRIES leading in **INCLUSIVE EDUCATION** and **UNIVERSAL EARLY INTERVENTION**

USA & UK strong in **RESEARCH, TECHNOLOGY**, and **NEURODIVERSITY EMPLOYMENT**

JAPAN & SOUTH KOREA feature **STRUCTURED SUPPORT** and **COMMUNITY INTEGRATION**

EMERGING ECONOMIES (e.g., India) create **INTEGRATED SYSTEMS** without **LEGACY FRAGMENTATION**

The goal is not to rank systems it is to recognize that **collective learning accelerates progress** for every family, in every country.

The Power of Policy Integration

One of the strongest lessons from global experience is this: **fragmented systems create fragmented outcomes.** When a child must navigate separate and disconnected healthcare, education, and social service systems, the burden falls entirely on the family to bridge the gaps.

Countries moving toward integrated policy frameworks reduce family burden significantly because the system takes responsibility for its own coherence, rather than expecting families to coordinate it alone. Integration is not a luxury. It is the structural foundation that determines whether support is real or merely symbolic.

The Emerging Global Direction

The conversation around autism is evolving beyond therapy alone toward the broader challenge of societal design. The future of autism support worldwide is taking shape around five interconnected priorities.

1

Lifecycle Planning

Support from early childhood through adulthood, without gap years

2

AI-Assisted Ecosystems

Intelligent tools that personalize and extend reach

3

Inclusive Infrastructure

Physical and digital spaces designed for diverse needs

4

Community-Centered Support

Local networks that surround and sustain families

> ⓘ This future will not emerge automatically. It must be built intentionally through policy, investment, collaboration, and sustained commitment across generations.

The Opportunity for Emerging Economies

Emerging nations including India occupy a uniquely powerful position in the global autism landscape. Rather than inheriting legacy systems built on outdated assumptions, they have the opportunity to build something better from the very beginning.

The Advantage of Starting Fresh

- Learn from global successes without repeating their mistakes
- Avoid institutional fragmentation from the outset
- Build integrated systems with modern technology as a foundation
- Leverage community and family structures already in place

Why This Matters Globally

Emerging economies represent the majority of the world's autistic population. The systems they build or fail to build will shape global outcomes more than any single developed nation's policy update.

The speed of progress in countries like India, Brazil, and across Sub-Saharan Africa will define the next chapter of the global autism story. Their success is the world's success.

The Need for Global Collaboration

Research, technology, and policy innovation should not remain isolated within national borders. Autism is not a local issue it is a human issue. The solutions that will transform lives are most likely to emerge when knowledge flows freely, ethically, and equitably across the world.

Knowledge Sharing

Open research partnerships that accelerate understanding across every continent

Best Practices

Disseminating what works in education, healthcare, and employment so no family starts from zero

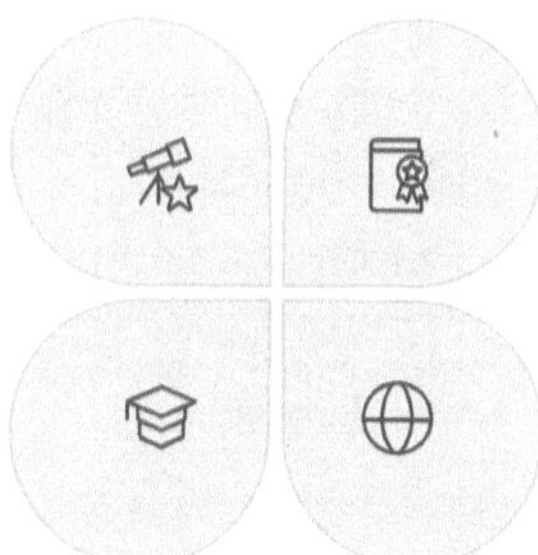

Inclusive Education Models

Sharing classroom innovations that work across cultural and resource contexts worldwide

Ethical AI Development

Building AI tools that are inclusive, transparent, and designed with diverse populations in mind from the start

A Future Beyond Fragmentation

Imagine a world where early support is universally accessible where inclusion is designed into systems from the start, where technology assists ethically, where employment pathways are normalized, and where families are continuously supported throughout the entire journey. This is not a utopian fantasy. It is a design challenge.

1

Universal Early Access

Every child, regardless of geography or income, receives timely identification and support

2

Inclusion by Design

Schools, workplaces, and communities built from the ground up to welcome neurodiversity

3

Ethical Technology

AI and digital tools that extend reach without replacing the human connection families need

4

Normalized Employment

Career pathways that recognize autistic talent and adapt structures to support contribution

5

Continuous Family Support

Systems that walk alongside families across every stage of life not just early childhood

A Final Reflection

The most powerful global lesson may be the simplest one: autism support improves when systems stop asking individuals to adapt alone and begin adapting collectively.

> The future of autism care will not belong to one country, one institution, or one technology. It will belong to ecosystems that combine intelligence, inclusion, and humanity.

Intelligence Without Inclusion Is Incomplete

The smartest systems in the world still fail families if they are not designed with equity, access, and human dignity at their center.

Inclusion Without Systems Cannot Scale

Compassion and goodwill alone cannot reach every family. Only well-designed, integrated, funded systems can deliver inclusion as a universal reality.

Humanity Is the Measure of All Progress

Whatever tools, policies, or frameworks the world builds their ultimate value is measured in the quality of life they create for autistic individuals and the families who love them.

The world has the knowledge. It now needs the will to build together.

EPILOGUE

From Awareness to Acceptance to Empowerment

Every journey changes the person who walks through it. And perhaps this journey changes society as well. This epilogue reflects on what it means to move beyond awareness toward a world where individuals with autism are not merely accommodated but empowered to participate, contribute, grow, and thrive with dignity.

A Shift in Understanding

For many years, the conversation around autism remained limited. The focus was often narrow diagnosis, deficits, and correction. The goal was frequently to make individuals appear "normal." But gradually, the world has begun to shift.

Then	Now	The Truth
Diagnosis-first. Deficit-focused. Aimed at conformity.	Toward understanding, inclusion, and neurodiversity.	Autism is a different way of experiencing the world not a condition to merely be managed.

This shift matters deeply. It reframes the entire conversation not as a problem to solve, but as a dimension of human experience to understand and support.

What This Journey Explored

Throughout this book, we examined the many dimensions of life with autism from the deeply personal to the broadly systemic. At the heart of every chapter lies one central idea: **human dignity**.

The Emotional Journey

The lived experiences of parents, families, and individuals navigating uncertainty with love and resilience.

Therapies & Education

The role of evidence-based approaches in supporting growth, learning, and connection.

Daily Life & Independence

The realities of adulthood, autonomy, and building a life that is meaningful and self-directed.

Technology & the Future

AI, integrated platforms, and personalized interventions shaping what is possible for generations ahead.

Autism Challenges Systems Not Just Individuals

Perhaps the most important lesson is this: autism does not only challenge individuals   it challenges systems. It asks us all to do better.

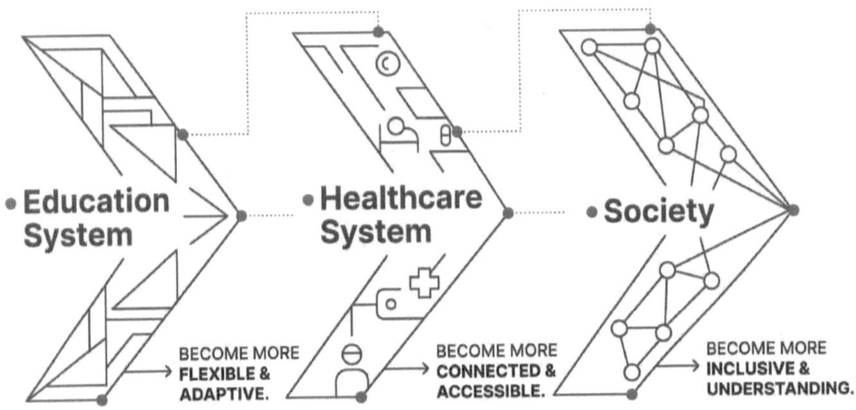

And in doing so, it pushes humanity toward a deeper understanding of itself. Progress is happening awareness is growing, conversations are evolving, and systems are beginning to adapt. For the first time, we are beginning to move beyond isolated interventions toward **holistic ecosystems of support**.

The Destination: Empowerment

Awareness is the beginning. Acceptance is the next step. But **empowerment is the destination.** Even as technology reshapes what is possible, one truth must remain unchanged: empathy cannot be automated. Human connection remains essential.

To Parents

Your consistency, patience, and love matter more than perfection ever will. Your journey is seen.

To Educators & Therapists

Your work reaches far beyond classrooms and sessions. One moment of understanding can change the direction of a life.

To Policymakers & Innovators

The future is not only about building smarter systems it is about building *humane* systems.

To Individuals on the Spectrum

Difference is not deficiency. Your way of seeing, feeling, and understanding the world matters profoundly.

> In the end, autism is not only about understanding one group of people differently. It is about learning to understand humanity more deeply and that understanding, combined with empathy, inclusion, and action, has the power to transform lives and the world we build together.

Reference

A curated, multi-domain bibliography supporting rigorous scholarship in autism, neurodevelopment, inclusion, and emerging technologies. This reference architecture spans foundational clinical texts, neuroscience research, global health policy, India-specific legislation, therapeutic frameworks, and AI ethics organized to guide clinicians, researchers, policymakers, and educators toward authoritative sources across every dimension of the field.

Foundational, Clinical & Scientific Sources

A. Foundational Autism Texts

- American Psychiatric Association *DSM-5-TR*
- Temple Grandin *The Autistic Brain*
- Barry M. Prizant *Uniquely Human*
- Steve Silberman *NeuroTribes*
- Tony Attwood *The Complete Guide to Asperger's Syndrome*
- Uta Frith *Autism: Explaining the Enigma*

B. Neuroscience & Developmental Research

- Simon Baron-Cohen *The Essential Difference*
- Schopler & Mesibov *Learning and Cognition in Autism*
- Catherine Lord et al. Diagnostic & developmental studies
- *Journal of Autism and Developmental Disorders*
- *Autism Research Journal*
- *The Lancet Neurology*

C. Global Health Organizations

- World Health Organization
- Centers for Disease Control and Prevention
- Autism Speaks
- National Autistic Society
- UNESCO
- UNICEF

D. India-Specific Policy & Institutional References

- Ministry of Social Justice and Empowerment
- Rehabilitation Council of India
- NIEPID National Institute for Empowerment of Persons with Intellectual Disabilities
- Rights of Persons with Disabilities (RPWD) Act
- National Education Policy (NEP) 2020
- Inclusive education guidelines from CBSE & NCERT

> ⓘ India's legislative and educational frameworks represent a critical policy layer for practitioners working within South Asian contexts. The RPWD Act and NEP 2020 together signal a meaningful shift toward rights-based, inclusive approaches in both welfare and schooling systems.

Cross-referencing these institutional sources with WHO frameworks and the DSM-5-TR ensures clinical and policy alignment at both national and international levels.

Therapeutic, Inclusion & Emerging Technology References

The following domains bridge intervention science, neurodiversity advocacy, and cutting-edge AI ethics forming the interdisciplinary foundation for contemporary, future-oriented autism scholarship.

E. Education & Inclusion

- Carol Gray *Social Stories & Comic Strip Conversations*
- Paula Kluth *You're Going to Love This Kid!*
- TEACCH Autism Program resources
- Universal Design for Learning (UDL) frameworks
- Inclusive classroom research literature

F. Therapy & Communication

- PECS Picture Exchange Communication System
- AAC communication frameworks
- Sensory Integration A. Jean Ayres
- ABA literature & modern critiques
- DIR/Floortime Developmental Relationship-Based Interventions

G. Neurodiversity & Inclusion

- Judy Singer Neurodiversity concept
- Nick Walker Neurodiversity Paradigm
- Disability inclusion & accessibility literature
- Human rights frameworks in disability inclusion

H. AI, Technology & Future Systems

A distinctive strength of this reference structure is its integration of AI ethics and assistive technology literature positioning autism scholarship within the broader horizon of digital health innovation.

- IEEE AI Ethics Guidelines
- UNESCO AI Ethics Recommendations
- Human-centered AI research papers
- Digital therapeutics research
- Assistive technology & wearable systems literature

I. Economics, Policy & System Design

Systems-level change demands grounding in public health economics and community-based models of care.

- Disability economics studies
- Inclusive workforce research
- WHO disability inclusion frameworks
- Public health systems integration research
- Community-based rehabilitation (CBR) models

This reference architecture is intentionally cross-disciplinary. Scholars and practitioners are encouraged to draw from multiple sections simultaneously pairing, for example, neuroscience research (Section B) with neurodiversity advocacy (Section G) and AI ethics (Section H) to build genuinely integrative, human-centered work.

www.ingramcontent.com/pod-product-compliance
Lightning Source LLC
LaVergne TN
LVHW100251210926
848480LV00003B/899